Biographies, Exhibition Histories,
and Bibliographies
by Anna Brooke

Published for the
Hirshhorn Museum and Sculpture Garden
by the Smithsonian Institution Press
Washington, D.C.

DIFFERENT DRUMMERS

Frank Gettings

Wallace Berman

Clyde Connell

Bruce Conner

Öyvind Fahlström

Robert Helm

Alfred Jensen

Jess

Luis Jimenez

Peter Saul

May 12–August 14, 1988
Hirshhorn Museum and Sculpture Garden
Smithsonian Institution

This book was edited by B.J. Bradley, designed by
Alan Carter, typeset in Bembo and Univers by VIP Systems, Inc.,
and printed on Warren Lustro Dull by Garamond Pridemark Press, Inc.

First edition

LIBRARY OF CONGRESS CATALOGING-IN-PUBLICATION DATA

Gettings, Frank.
   Different drummers.

   Exhibition held on May 12–Aug. 14, 1988,
Hirshhorn Museum and Sculpture Garden.
   Bibliography: p.
   1. Art, American—Themes, motives—Exhibitions.
2. Art, Modern—20th century—United States—Themes,
motives—Exhibitions. I. Brooke, Anna. II. Berman,
Wallace, 1926-1976. III. Hirshhorn Museum and
Sculpture Garden. IV. Title.
N6512.G44   1988   709′.73′0740153   87-43339
ISBN 0-87474-471-7

Contents

Lenders to the Exhibition

Stephen S. Alpert
Sharon Avery-Fahlström
Elizabeth B. Blake, Dallas
Laura L. Carpenter, Dallas
Edward R. Downe, Jr., New York
Mr. and Mrs. Klaus Groenke, Berlin
Mr. and Mrs. Graham Gund, Cambridge, Massachusetts
Wendy and Alan Hart, Topanga, California
Dennis Hopper, Los Angeles
The Peter Jensen Trust, New York
Ed and Nancy Kienholz, Hope, Idaho
Dan and Barbara Lincove, Shreveport, Louisiana
Mr. and Mrs. Alan M. May, Dallas
Mr. and Mrs. S.I. Newhouse, Jr., New York
Roger H. Ogden, New Orleans
Mr. and Mrs. George Perutz, Dallas
Frank Ribelin, Dallas
Rodney Sheldon, Beverly Hills, California
Martin Sklar, New York
Randall Timmons, New Orleans
Nicholas Wilder, New York
Richard S. Zeisler, New York
Private collections

Dallas Museum of Art
Hirshhorn Museum and Sculpture Garden, Smithsonian Institution,
        Washington, D.C.
James C. Bolton Library, Louisiana State University at Alexandria
The Jewish Museum, New York
Krannert Art Museum, University of Illinois, Champaign
Los Angeles County Museum of Art
Metropolitan Museum of Art, New York
Moderna Museet, Stockholm
The Museum of Modern Art, New York
National Museum of American Art, Smithsonian Institution,
        Washington, D.C.
San Francisco Museum of Modern Art
Solomon R. Guggenheim Museum, New York
Tyler Museum of Art, Tyler, Texas
Whitney Museum of American Art, New York

The Candy Store Gallery, Folsom, California
Frumkin/Adams Gallery, New York
Sidney Janis Gallery, New York
Phyllis Kind Gallery, New York and Chicago
L.A. Louver, Venice, California
Moody Gallery, Houston
Odyssia Gallery, New York
Edward Thorp Gallery, New York

Foreword

The herd mentality in the visual arts—especially, though not exclusively, in the art of the past one hundred years—has been a phenomenon that even the casual observer will have noted.

An artistic movement that may have its origins in honest and profound intellectual and philosophical attitudes can rapidly become an innocuous cliché as it spreads geographically from its core and as the passage of time blurs the clarity and meaning of its original state. To cite one example, as the Impressionism of Monet and his friends became astonishingly popular, it quickly was misunderstood. Its vigor and freshness were soon dissipated on the easels of countless camp followers on both sides of the Atlantic and, as the decades passed, in Paris itself. One need not ponder long to conjure up more recent examples where fashion has played a debilitating role.

Fashion, however, is not the realm of the nine artists represented in this exhibition. Nor should they be considered deliberately nonconformist, which would imply a calculated "strategy" to be different for its own sake— a fashionable posture to assume these days. They are what they are.

In addition to their indifference to current trends of taste, these artists, like Thoreau at Walden Pond, are isolated—geographically, psychologically, and artistically. For many years Alfred Jensen lived and worked in New York City, the country's overcrowded art capital. But his obsession with numerological systems, with Goethe's color theories, and with Leonardo's often inscrutable writings separated him in his work and thoughts as surely as living far from the traditional centers of artistic creativity has set Clyde Connell and Robert Helm apart.

Originality is the hallmark of these artists and it is their uniqueness that frustrates and defies the art historian's abiding need for categorization. Several of them were included in various early publications and exhibitions of Pop Art, but today, twenty-five years later, these inclusions appear to have been critical and curatorial errors. Perhaps even this exhibition, although it presents diverse work by nine mavericks, is too restrictive an environment. For these artists remain individualists to the core.

Although the lenders to the exhibition are acknowledged elsewhere in this catalog, I, too, wish to extend my heartfelt thanks to them. By their collecting they have shown their own independence.

It is a healthy and encouraging sign that the list of artists who could have been included here is a lengthy and distinguished one. My gratitude goes to curator Frank Gettings for making the selection and for organizing the exhibition under circumstances that were often difficult and trying.

James T. Demetrion
Director
Hirshhorn Museum and Sculpture Garden

Acknowledgments

Selecting artists whose work is outside the mainstream of contemporary art was a challenge, and to the many people all across the country who helped me in my search, I extend my thanks.

Peter Goulds, director of L.A. Louver in Los Angeles, and his associate director, Annette Andersen, provided considerable assistance in my research on works by both Wallace Berman and Robert Helm; information on the latter artist also came from Edward Thorp and his gallery in New York. Becoming familiar with Clyde Connell's sculpture would have been impossible without help from David Connelly of the *Shreveport Journal* in Louisiana; the Barry Whistler Gallery in Dallas; Arthur Roger in New Orleans; and, in New York, the Damon Brandt Gallery and the Oscarsson Siegeltuch Gallery.

Advice about the works of Öyvind Fahlström was given by his widow Sharon Avery-Fahlström and Arnold Herstand and his gallery in New York, as well as Carroll and Conrad Janis of the Sidney Janis Gallery in New York. Peter Boris at the Pace Gallery, New York, and Maria Reidelbach of the Peter Jensen Trust, also in New York, provided information on Alfred Jensen's paintings. Valuable information about Jess and his art was freely offered by Odyssia Skouras and Federico Quadrani of Odyssia Gallery in New York.

Information on Luis Jimenez was made available to me by Betty Moody and her gallery assistant, Lisa Barkley, of the Betty Moody Gallery in Houston, and Carol Celantano of the Phyllis Kind Gallery in New York. George Smith, director of the Frumkin/Adams Gallery in New York, helped me gather material on Peter Saul.

I want to thank Sharon Corgan Leeber of the Architectural Arts Company in Dallas who drove me from that city to the shores of Lake Bistineau and back to visit Clyde Connell and the Tyler Museum. Dayna Johnson guided me to various museums and galleries in Houston and environs. Jane Whitney showed me the Edward Janss collection and art galleries in the Los Angeles area. I also want to thank Michel Feuche for his insights and observations about this show.

Staff members in several museums also played an integral part in the organization of this exhibition, including Sue Graze, curator of contemporary art, and Elizabeth Simon, curatorial assistant, Dallas Museum of Art; Carol Rosset, registrar, and Anita C. Gross, registration assistant, San Francisco Museum of Modern Art; Alexandra Musek, loan assistant, and Lynn Addison, associate registrar, Museum of Modern Art in New York; Anita Duquette, rights and reproductions manager, Whitney Museum of American Art in New York; and Cornelia Lauf, curatorial assistant, Solomon R. Guggenheim Museum in New York.

From the very beginning Hirshhorn Museum and Sculpture Garden Director James T. Demetrion enthusiastically encouraged my efforts. Deputy Director Stephen E. Weil gave assistance on many aspects of the exhibition and catalog. Chief Curator for Exhibitions Ned Rifkin helped me focus my search. Financial issues were ably handled by Executive Officer Nancy F. Kirkpatrick. Although burdened by a busy schedule, B.J. Bradley, the museum's editor, orchestrated all efforts concerning the catalog's development. Jennifer Loviglio devoted much time to many aspects of the exhibition, from sending out loan forms to organizing checklists and documents.

Nancy Kaiser made my travel arrangements across the country, and Dorothy Valakos typed much of my correspondence. Carolyn Lewis, the museum's receptionist, handled the many messages and express packages concerning this exhibition. Jim Mahoney helped me manipulate the word processor and counseled me in aspects of the tarot card reference appearing in a work by Jess. Public Affairs Officer Sidney Lawrence and his assistant Dale Vanderheyden enthusiastically informed the media about the show, and Carol Parsons, special events officer, coordinated all matters relating to the exhibition preview.

To Ed Schiesser, Bob Allen, and the other members of the Exhibits and Design department, who designed and installed the exhibition with their usual skill, and to Assistant Registrar for Exhibitions Barbara Freund, who efficiently arranged transportation for the works of art, I am very grateful.

Producing this catalog involved the efforts of many professionals. I am indebted to the museum's Chief Photographer Lee Stalsworth and his assistant Marianne Gurley for their excellent work. Together with her staff, Librarian Anna Brooke organized each artist's biography, exhibition history, and bibliography. The Smithsonian Institution Press provided valuable help in the services of Michelle K. Smith, editor, and Alan Carter, designer.

Finally I would like to express my gratitude, and the museum's, to the artists and to the lenders who have generously agreed to live without their objects for the duration of the show. Such cooperation and interest made this venture a success, for these splendid works by different drummers have justified my search.

Frank Gettings

Different Drummers

Among the lines in Henry David Thoreau's *Walden* are these:

> *If a man does not keep pace with his companions, perhaps it is because he hears a different drummer. Let him step to the music which he hears, however measured or far away.*[1]

Thoreau's reference to individuals whose expression is personal and outside the mainstream is now a well-understood idiom in the American language. It is used here to describe paintings, sculptures, and drawings by nine contemporary artists whose work cannot be easily categorized within current groups or tendencies in contemporary art.

Since World War II, art movements have both rocked and stimulated the art world in quick succession. The artists in this exhibition are among those who have balanced these popular "hysterias" against their own beliefs about what is universal and timeless. Clearly, many artists use forms of expression that differ sharply from those of most of their peers or from what the art world accepts, but this exhibition is not meant to be an encyclopedic collection of different drummers. The selection was governed by the physical limits of the museum's exhibition space and by the need to show more than one example of each artist's work in order to represent clearly, and fairly, their aims, ambitions, and beliefs.

Individual artists with different, even controversial, ideas and styles of expression have existed throughout the centuries. Hieronymus Bosch (1450?–1516) painted in exquisite detail unusual plants, animals, and diabolical figures. When studied carefully or turned upside-down, the paintings of fruits and vegetables by Giuseppe Arcimboldo (1530–93) become human faces. Francisco Goya (1746–1828) created strange and caustic etchings. Because his work mysteriously evoked the dream world, Odilon Redon (1840–1916) was considered one of the precursors of Surrealism. Albert Pinkham Ryder (1847–1917) obsessively reworked, often for years, paintings that expressed the enigmatic forces of nature in rhythmic and somber masses. And Antonio Gaudí (1852–1926) designed bizarre yet startlingly elegant architectural forms.

Eccentric visual statements began to appear in contemporary art in the United States (especially on the West Coast) in the 1950s and 1960s when symbolism and social consciousness began to merge to convey a reaction, which had Surrealist overtones, to the atomic bomb and the U.S. military presence in Southeast Asia. During this period, it was taken for granted by the art world that art could not be associated with political events and social problems. Yet many artists lost their political innocence at that time and looked for ways to release their slowly fermenting frustration.

1. Henry David Thoreau, *Walden*. (1854; Philadelphia: Running Press, 1987), 192.

Concern for the destruction of humanity can be seen in the surreal horrific objects that Bruce Conner constructed of sinister-looking materials. The late Wallace Berman created objects and collages that expressed his dislike for the complacent, hypocritical attitude he thought had infected society. His works focus on the cruel and inhuman treatment of the Jews and other groups during the Second World War.

A fear of the government's actions and their consequences existed among other artists as well. On the other side of the country, in New York, the late Öyvind Fahlström developed charged images in drawings, paintings, and constructions that attacked what he felt were international manipulations by government agencies both here and abroad. Peter Saul saw a danger to American society in the violence of the Vietnam war as well as in the mindless violence that was becoming part of everyday existence. His satirical paintings have social, political, and sexual overtones forcefully presented in dramatic compositions with raw colors.

Conversely, personal and intellectual matters that had little to do with national or international issues obsessed some artists and led them to their distinctive styles. The late Alfred Jensen's interest in complex systems he believed he had discovered in ancient civilizations and his obsession with some of the mathematical formulas of modern science are the source of his fascinating paintings. He diagrammed his ideas on canvas with thick paint in hues governed by the color theories of Goethe, who pursued his scientific studies in terms of personal theories.

Robert Helm's intimate, enigmatic shadowboxes and paintings are self-referential. A strong sense of his experiences and things that have obsessed him inhabit his works, which are not narratives. Jess creates incredibly complex collages and heavily painted works on canvas; many are elaborate puns with literary sources.

The Hispanic-American artist Luis Jimenez uses popular culture as well as ancient myths as source material for his sculptures and drawings. A concern for humanity and nature in a high-tech environment impels Clyde Connell to create sculptural sanctuaries—altars and places that she feels welcome people into their comfortable presence.

Several of these artists enter into a mental dialogue with the materials that fashion their ideas. Jess feels that the collage he is working on guides his hand. Clyde Connell wants a sculpture to assume its own identity (or function) gradually, while she is creating it. Seemingly to match their singular ideas, many have chosen to use nontraditional art materials, which have become their signatures. Wallace Berman used an early photocopying process; the basic structure of many of Clyde Connell's sculptures is papier mâché and wood; Bruce Conner uses nylon stocking to convey an atmosphere of mystery and fear; Luis Jimenez creates sculpture with fiberglass and colorful acrylic spray paint.

Consistent with each artist's attitude, works of art are not produced impulsively; all approach their work carefully and deliberately. Robert Helm's knowledge of exotic woods and his ability to carve inform his wall constructions, paintings, and frames. Jess's collages are made from hundreds of pieces of printed images carefully cut from publications and then pinned to the surface of a support to be slowly studied before being glued in their proper place. The skills that Luis Jimenez learned in his father's sign shop continue to enhance his sculpture.

In their art these nine artists focus on personal, often mystical, obsessions and concerns. Using styles that range from gentle introspection to hard-hitting brutality, they present ideas in highly complex and personal ways instead of reflecting purely formalistic interests in composition and color. Their unusual approaches to creating paintings, drawings, and sculptures place these artists outside the mainstream of contemporary art.

Frank Gettings
Curator of Prints and Drawings

Catalog of the Exhibition

Dimensions are given in inches, height preceding width preceding depth. Media and dimensions are given as supplied by lenders. Figures in parentheses refer to catalog numbers.

—

Wallace Berman

Wallace Berman's works, which have strong moral and spiritual overtones, stem from what he believed were the social and ethical hypocrisies of the post-World War II era. His concerns included the fate of the Jewish people during the Holocaust. His works should not be read as literal statements or narratives but as associative metaphors about the world as he saw it.

Although he was not widely known, he became a major link among many artists, poets, musicians, and writers. He knew and corresponded with Jess and his poet companion Robert Duncan. Berman's first exhibition at the Ferus Gallery (1957) in San Francisco was closed by the police because one of the works was considered lewd and lascivious. When convicted at a juryless trial, he stated aloud to his courtroom audience, "There is no justice, just revenge."[1] Berman produced no art for exhibition from 1957 to 1964, when he began his first series of collages using a Verifax photocopier. His interests embraced both art and music. He had attended Chouinard Art Institute and Jepson Art Institute, and he wrote rhythm-and-blues with Jimmy Witherspoon. In 1955 Berman started *Semina*, a largely handmade magazine that ran for nine issues and had a small, select readership. In 1960 he opened an art gallery named after the magazine. Berman died in 1976 in an automobile accident.

The Hebrew letters Berman put on rocks, parchment, and pictures cannot be translated into understandable words or sentences. Artifacts of a lost language, the letters evoke moods and feelings and are thought to have secret meanings, not unlike those in the cabala, an ancient esoteric interpretation of Hebrew scriptures. No one who knew Berman thought that a key to their meaning ever existed that would make his message obvious. Yet his letters need no translation because their very existence conveys the sense of mysticism that governed much of his work.

The large Hebrew letters of *Untitled*, c. 1956–57 (1), appear to have been stenciled on ancient papyrus. Walter Hopps, who together with Ed Kienholz owned Ferus Gallery where these untitled works were first exhibited, has called them "the Witnesses." "Wallace himself spoke of the stream of consciousness. He said to me, 'I'm letting it come through from dead Poets.' These were the Witnesses."[2]

Guillaume Apollinaire once suggested that poets should model their work on the omnipresent daily newspaper, "which, on a single sheet, treats the most diverse matters and ranges over distant countries."[3] Berman combined mass-media printed images with twentieth-century technology by affixing cards showing different scenes to the speaker of a pocket radio. Among the images he used to make his "radio cards" are pictures of snakes, animals, mushrooms, religious leaders, football and basketball players, and cosmic scenes. In two large Verifax collages from 1967 (4,5) Berman arranged a series of radio cards in a grid. The effect is similar to an encyclopedic rebus of "diverse matters." In two other Verifax collages (3, 8) the radio cards seem about to be shuffled like a deck of tarot cards. Taken together, the images suggest ideas and events current in the 1960s: the gun could refer to President John Kennedy's assassination; the mushrooms to psychedelic drugs; the religious leaders and emblems to a generation's search for life's meaning; the surgeon to the first heart transplant. And the mandala and mushroom on a stem have strong erotic overtones.

The images in Berman's collages thus reflect spiritual and worldly concerns, some violent, some harmonious. His choice of a hand-held radio is a symbol for the intimate message his works transmit. The arena or sheet of paper on which he presents his message is itself a paper specially made to duplicate images so that they can be seen by a wider audience. The substance of his work is a cavalcade of the sixties. Through it the viewer gets a sense of the events and ideas Berman thought important.

1. "An Interview with Walter Hopps," in *Wallace Berman: Retrospective* (Los Angeles: Otis Art Institute, 1978), 11.

2. Ibid., 9.

3. In William Seitz, *The Art of Assemblage* (New York: Museum of Modern Art, 1961), 74.

1
Untitled, 1956–57
Ink on parchment; 19½ x 19½ inches
Ed and Nancy Kienholz, Hope, Idaho

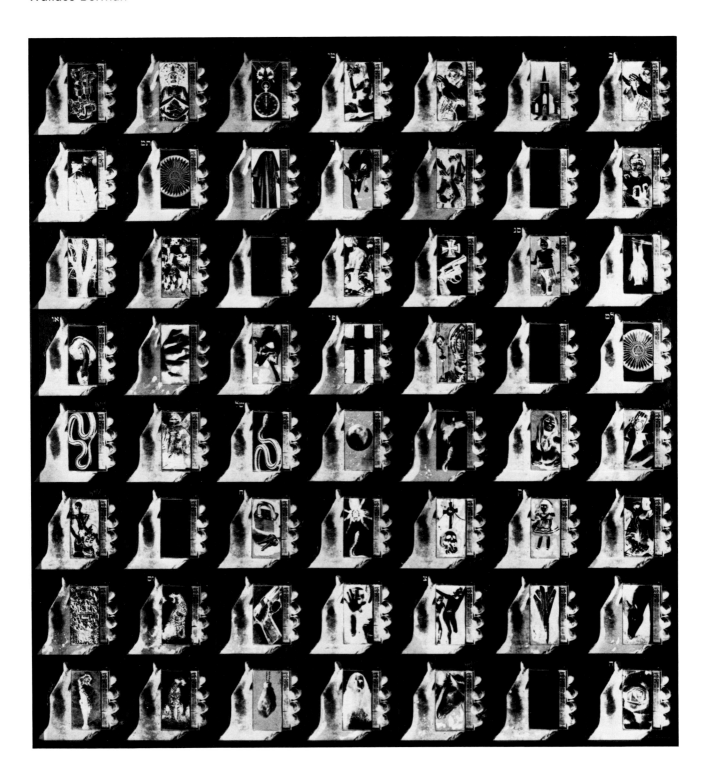

2
Untitled, 1964
Verifax collage; 47½ x 45⅛ inches
Dallas Museum of Art, General Acquisitions Fund

3
Scope, 1965
Verifax collage; 38 x 22 inches
Dennis Hopper, Los Angeles

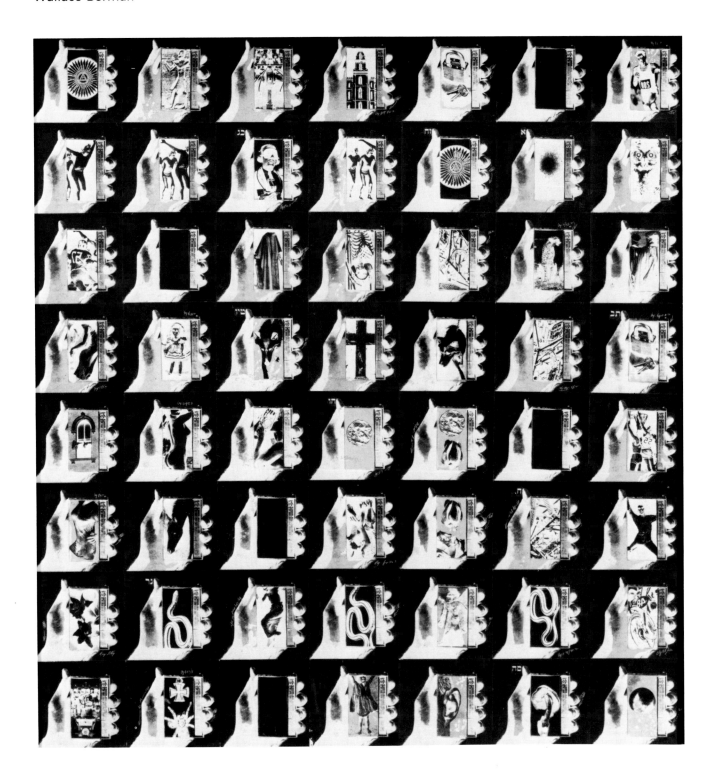

4
Untitled, 1967
Verifax collage; 46¾ x 49¼ inches
Courtesy L.A. Louver, Venice, California

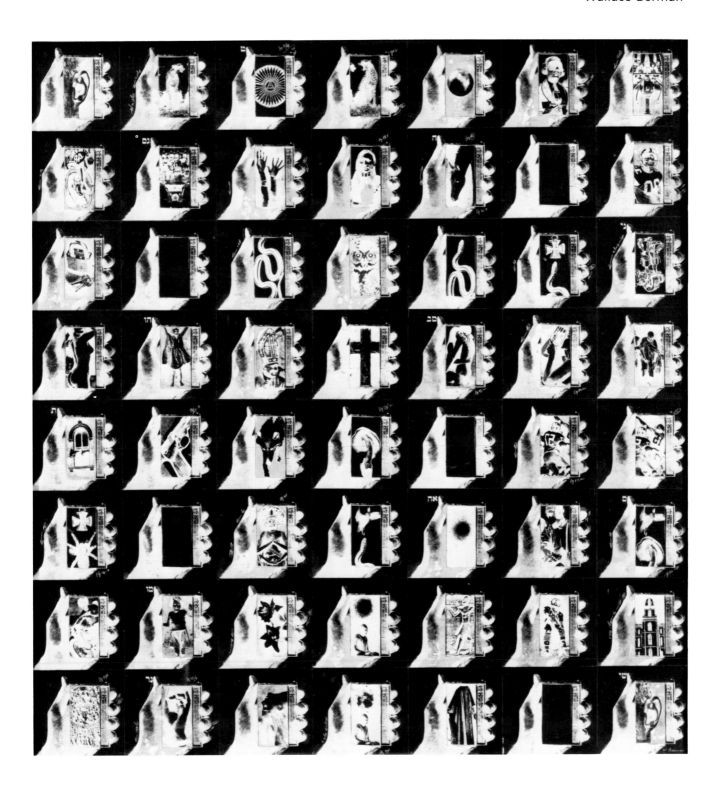

5
Untitled, 1967
Verifax collage; 46¾ x 49¼ inches
Courtesy L.A. Louver, Venice, California

6
Untitled, 1967
Verifax collage and acrylic; 13 x 14 inches
Rodney Sheldon, Beverly Hills, California, courtesy L.A. Louver, Venice, California

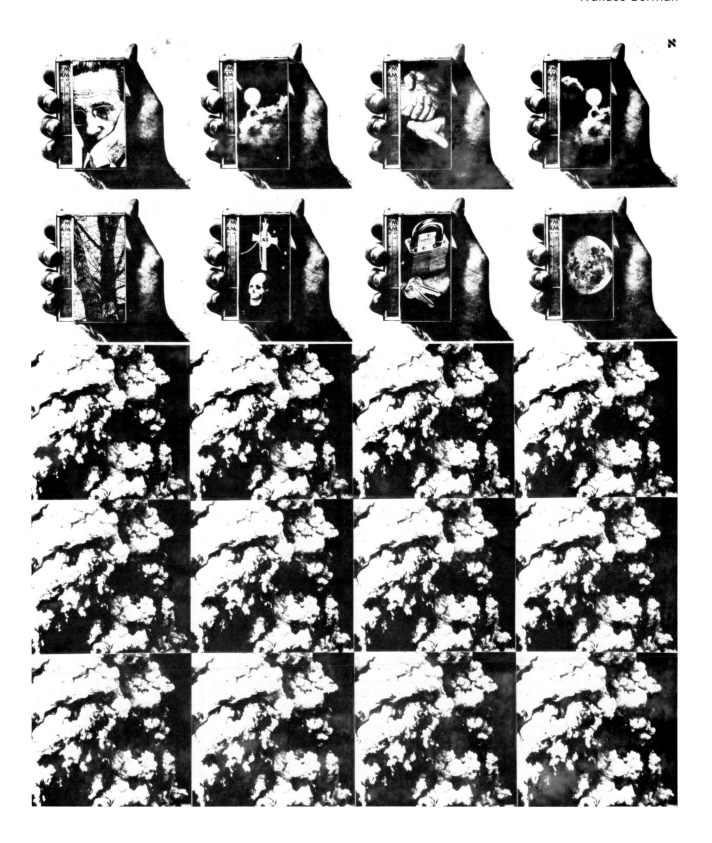

7
Untitled, c. 1969
Verifax collage; 29⅝ x 26 inches
Dallas Museum of Art, anonymous gift in honor of Mr. and Mrs. Robert A. White

8
Untitled, 1969
Verifax collage and acrylic; 13 x 14 inches
Private collection, courtesy L.A. Louver, Venice, California

9
Untitled, 1972
Stones, paint, wood, screws, photographs, and plexiglass; 9½ x 13½ x 6½ inches
The Jewish Museum, New York

10
Untitled (400.300.50), 1974
Acrylic on rock with chain; 5¾ x 7⅝ x 7⅝ inches
San Francisco Museum of Modern Art

Wallace Berman, 1963–65

Biography

Born Wallace Berman, February 18, 1926, in Staten Island, New York. Education: Chouinard Art Institute, Los Angeles, 1944, and Jepson Art Institute, Los Angeles, 1945. Worked in a furniture factory, 1948–50. Published *Semina* magazine, 1955–64. Awards include: William and Noma Copley Foundation Award, 1965; National Council on the Arts and Humanities Grant, 1966. Died February 18, 1976, in Topanga Canyon, California.

Selected Solo Exhibitions

1957
Ferus Gallery, Los Angeles, *Wallace Berman*, June 7–July 4.

1965
Beverly Glen, Los Angeles, *Studio Exhibition*, October 10–17.

1967
Topanga Community House, Topanga, Calif., February 26.

1968
Los Angeles County Museum of Art, *Wallace Berman*, April 30–June 2.
Jewish Museum, New York, *Wallace Berman: Verifax Collages*, September 17–
    November 17.

1973
Mermaid Tavern, Topanga, Calif., *Exhibition/Wallace Berman*, June 9.

1977
Timothea Stewart Gallery, Los Angeles, *Wallace Berman*, July–August.

1978
Whitney Museum of American Art, New York, *Wallace Berman*, January 18–March 5.
Otis Art Institute Gallery, Los Angeles, *Wallace Berman Retrospective*, October 24–
    November 26, and tour to Fort Worth (Tex.) Art Museum, January 10–February 18,
    1979; University Art Museum, University of California, Berkeley, September 21–
    November 11; Seattle Art Museum, December 13–January 27, 1980.

1982
Charles Cowles Gallery, New York, *Wallace Berman*, March 4–27.

Wallace Berman

Selected Group Exhibitions

1966
Robert Fraser Gallery, London, *Los Angeles Now,* January 31–February 19.

1968
Art Gallery, University of California, Irvine, *Assemblage in California,* October 15–November 24.
Los Angeles County Museum of Art, *The Late Fifties at Ferus,* November 12–December 17.

1969
Hayward Gallery, London, *Pop Art Redefined,* July 9–September 3.
Pasadena (Calif.) Art Museum, *West Coast 1945–1969,* November 24–January 18, 1970.

1974
Dallas Museum of Fine Arts and Pollock Galleries, Southern Methodist University, Dallas, *Poets of the Cities: New York and San Francisco 1950–1965,* November 20–December 29, and tour to San Francisco Museum of Modern Art, January 31–March 23, 1975; Wadsworth Atheneum, Hartford, Conn., April 23–June 1.

1975
Mount Holyoke College, South Hadley, Mass., *Art As a Muscular Principle/Ten Artists and San Francisco 1950–1965,* February 28–March 20.
Los Angeles Institute of Contemporary Art, *Collage and Assemblage,* April–May.
University of California, Davis, *Environment and the New Art 1960–1975,* November 12–December 18.

1976
Newport Harbor Art Museum, Newport Beach, Calif., *The Last Time I Saw Ferus 1957–1966,* March 7–April 17.
San Francisco Museum of Modern Art, *Painting and Sculpture in California: The Modern Era,* September 3–November 21, and tour to National Collection of Fine Arts, Washington, D.C., May 20–September 11, 1977.

1981
Los Angeles County Museum of Art, *Art in Los Angeles: Seventeen Artists in the Sixties,* July 21–October 4, and tour to San Antonio (Tex.) Museum of Art, November 20–January 31, 1982.
Laguna Beach (Calif.) Museum of Art, *Southern California Artists 1940–1980,* July 23–September 13.

1983
Gallery Paule Anglim, San Francisco, *Sight/Vision/The Urban Milieu,* October 5–November 5.

1987
University Art Museum, University of California, Berkeley, *Made in USA: An Americanization in Modern Art, the Fifties and Sixties,* April 4–June 21, and tour to Nelson-Atkins Museum of Art, Kansas City, Mo., July 25–September 6; Virginia Museum of Fine Arts, Richmond, October 7–December 7.

Selected Bibliography

Ayres, Anne Bartlett. "Berman and Kienholz: Progenitors of Los Angeles Assemblage," in *Art in Los Angeles: Seventeen Artists in the Sixties.* Exhibition catalog. Los Angeles: Los Angeles County Museum of Art, 1981, pp. 11–18.

Coplans, John. "Art Is Love Is God." *Artforum* 2 (March 1964): 26–27. Excerpt reprinted in *Assemblage in California.* Exhibition catalog. Irvine: University of California, 1968, p. 8.

———. "Circle of Styles on the West Coast." *Art in America* 52, no. 3 (June 1964): 24–41.

———. "Los Angeles Object Lesson." *Art News* 64 (January 1966): 40, 67.

Greene, Merril. "Wallace Berman," in *Art As a Muscular Principle/Ten Artists and San Francisco 1950–1965*. Exhibition catalog. South Hadley, Mass.: Mount Holyoke College, 1975, pp. 50–53.

———. "Wallace Berman: Portrait of the Artist As Underground Man." *Artforum* 16 (February 1978): 53–61.

Herms, George. Introduction to *Wallace Berman*. Exhibition brochure. Los Angeles: Timothea Stewart Gallery, 1977.

Larsen, Susan C. "Los Angeles, Have You Met Dick Nixon?" *Art News* 78 (February 1979): 140–44.

Livingston, Jane. "Two Generations in L.A." *Art in America* 57 (January 1969): 92–97.

Schjeldahl, Peter. "Wallace Berman at Otis Art Institute." *Art in America* 67 (March 1979): 156.

Simon, Rita. "Wallace Berman: Verifax Collages." *Arts Magazine* 43 (November 1968): 53.

Solnit, Rebecca. "Connections with the Past." *Artweek* 16 (April 20, 1985): 4–5.

Van Proyen, Mark. "Sight/Vision: The Inward Gaze." *Artweek* 14 (October 29, 1983): 1, 16.

Wallace Berman: Retrospective. Exhibition catalog. Los Angeles: Otis Art Institute Gallery, 1978. Texts by Hal Glickman, Robert Duncan, and David Meltzer. Interview with Walter Hopps.

Wallace Berman: Verifax Collages. Exhibition brochure. New York: Jewish Museum, 1978. Text by James Monte.

Wolfe, Clair. "Wallace Berman: A Seminal Influence." *Umbrella* 2 (January 1979): 1–2.

Wortz, Melinda. "Los Angeles: The Zen-Science of Light." *Art News* 76 (November 1977): 200–6.

Clyde Connell

Clyde Connell's sculpture is closely allied with nature's cyclical processes—birth, life, and death—and it conveys a sense of the pantheistic doctrines identifying nature with God. Made from the natural materials that surround her home and studio, her works project the sounds and rhythms of that solitary place on the edge of Lake Bistineau (near Shreveport, Louisiana). Her enigmatic sculptures are communicating presences describing primitive rituals for healing and protection.

Born on a plantation in the Bossier Parish community of Belcher, Louisiana, Connell grew up hearing stories about the Civil War. She studied art at Breneau College in Gainsville, Georgia, and in the 1950s she attended art classes at the Louisiana State Museum and began to visit New York museums and art galleries. "I was so influenced in the 1950s by Abstract Expressionists like Pollock, Motherwell, and Gottlieb."[1] In 1959 she moved from Shreveport to Lake Bistineau, whose fertile ambiance brought her closer to the visible and audible processes of nature that influence her art.

"While examining the nests of insects and moths around the lake I began to realize the mixture of paper, glue, and plastic [that I used] had a quality related to the material used to build dirt dobber, wasp, and moth nests."[2] Many of her pieces have an infrastructure of wood covered with a mulch made from bark, making a kind of papier mâché. It, in turn, is varnished with multiple layers of polyurethane. Before varnishing, Connell often pounds tacks into the surface, which eventually acquires the bumpy texture of the bark of the hackberry trees that surround her house and studio. Indigenous rattan vines, rocks, and pebbles are often found in her sculpture.

Asked why she started to create these sculptures she said, "This place has to have sculpture. . . . I wanted something that was like a connection between the earth and the moss . . . and so the vertical sculptures were made."[3] Her works can be appreciated on many different levels, from their pleasing proportion and scale to the sense that they have a ritualistic purpose. The Guardians are protective patriarchal figures, austere like silent sentinels and often larger than human figures. While the Guardians may intimidate, works from the Habitat series invite and nurture. Connell says she "wanted to create a ritual, protected place of the kind that animals and people always make for themselves in nature."[4]

Niches in the Habitat series are like sanctuaries. The focus of *Habitat I,* 1977 (12), is a womb that contains three altar objects—a red metal disc surmounted by two metal objects. Connell's Habitats have the character and innocence of primitive places that serve as reliquaries for offerings to the spirits of nature.

Made of rattan, *Rain Place,* 1978 (13), looks like a three-dimensional drawing in space. Although larger than most of her works, this piece is not massive. Its open lattice-like quality conveys a sense of movement. Just below the top of the frame is a row of three small openings or sanctuaries. Each contains a small stone and each has a vine ladder, but only tiny creatures can approach using those routes.

Non People Posts, 1978 (14), is composed of three stylized figures in positions similar to those found on medieval English tombs. Rings of metal from a piece of farm machinery create the featureless faces. Lengths of chain, rods, and other linear metal pieces help define the inert bodies. Other intricate forms and the variegated background of this wall piece are made from glued and laminated paper.

Clyde Connell's works take the form of mystic talismans or votive objects. Sculptural analogues for her compassion, her works express primal beliefs that are closely connected to the fecund environment of the land, mossy trees, and wildlife that surround her studio and home. The almost subliminal comfort her works exude instills in viewers a deeper understanding of what it means to be human and a need for a more meaningful spiritual life.

1. David Connelly, "Connell Works Set for Hirshhorn," *Shreveport Journal,* April 29, 1987, p. 4C.

2. Connell quoted in Ronald Watson, *Clyde Connell: Recent Paintings and Sculpture* (Fort Worth: Texas Christian University), n.p.

3. From a 1987 interview with the author.

4. *Clyde Connell, Recent Works* (Baton Rouge: Louisiana State University, 1985), n.p.

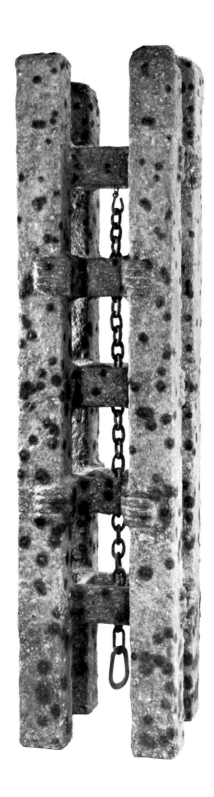

11
Gate of the South Wind, 1973
Mixed media; 75 x 28 x 20 inches
James C. Bolton Library, Louisiana State University at Alexandria

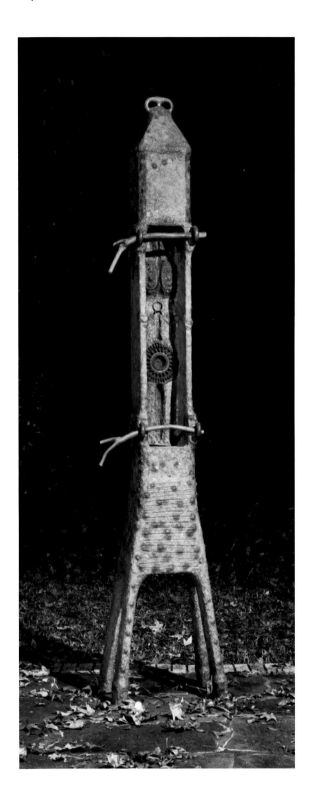

13
Rain Place, 1978
Mixed media; 84 x 54 x 36 inches
Laura L. Carpenter, Dallas

12
Habitat I, 1977
Mixed media; 86 x 17 x 15 inches
Dan and Barbara Lincove, Shreveport, Louisiana

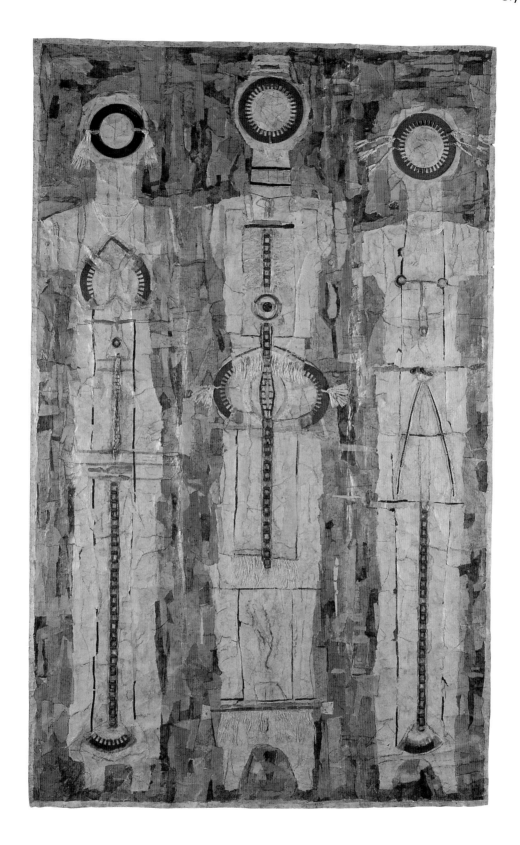

14
Non People Posts, 1978
Mixed media on paper; 108 x 67 inches
Dallas Museum of Art, Foundation for the Arts Collection, anonymous gift

15
Woods Habitat, 1978
Mixed media; 71 x 22 x 24 inches
Laura L. Carpenter, Dallas

16
Pondering Place, 1981
Mixed media; 80 x 25 x 25 inches
Roger H. Ogden, New Orleans

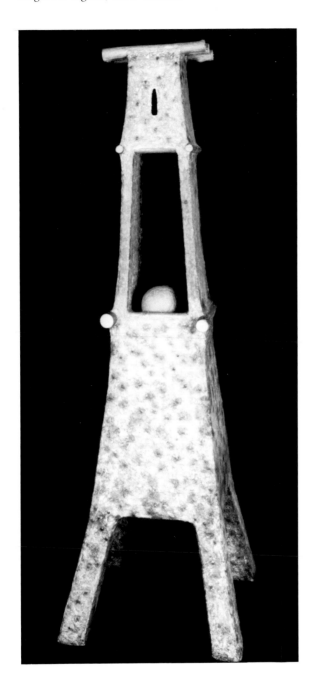

17
Sound Post I, 1981
Mixed media; 91 x 16 x 16 inches
Randall Timmons, New Orleans

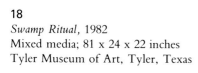

18
Swamp Ritual, 1982
Mixed media; 81 x 24 x 22 inches
Tyler Museum of Art, Tyler, Texas

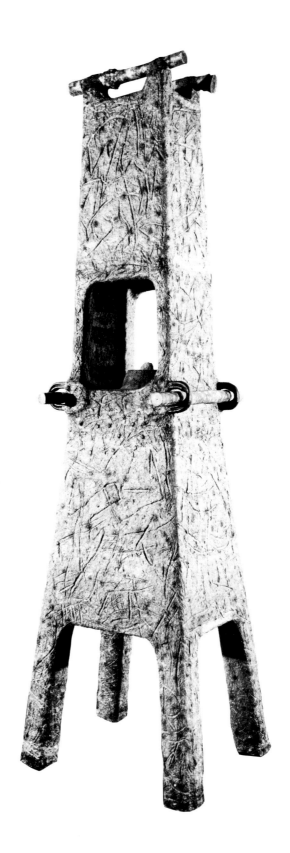

Clyde Connell, 1987

Biography

Born Clyde Dixon, September 19, 1901, in Belcher, Louisiana. Education: Breneau College, Gainsville, Georgia, 1918–19; Vanderbilt University, Nashville, Tennessee, 1919–20; Louisiana State Museum, Shreveport, 1950–55; Allison Well's Art Colony, Way, Mississippi, 1958. Awards include: Outstanding Achievement in the Visual Arts, Women's Caucus for Art, 1984. Honorary D.F.A. Centenary College of Louisiana, Shreveport, 1987. Lives and works in Elm Grove, Louisiana.

Selected Solo Exhibitions

1959
Friedenburg Artists' Loft, Shreveport, La., November 1–30.

1973
Library, Louisiana State University, Alexandria, *Clyde Connell,* April 8–May 8.

1979
Tyler (Tex.) Museum of Art, *An Exhibition of Works by Clyde Connell,* January 13–
    February 25.

1980
D.W. Gallery, Dallas, *Clyde Connell,* February 8–March 8.

1981
Barnwell Garden and Art Center, Shreveport, La., *Clyde Connell: Retrospective,* August 8–
    30.
The Clocktower, Institute for Art and Urban Resources, New York, *Clyde Connell,*
    November 11–December 12.

1982
Alexandria (La.) Museum, Visual Art Center, *Clyde Connell,* February 6–April 15.
Mississippi Museum of Art, Jackson, *Clyde Connell,* April 27–May 23.
Texas Christian University, Fort Worth, *Clyde Connell: Recent Paintings and Sculpture,*
    September 1–26.

1983
Delahunty Gallery, Dallas, *Clyde Connell: Recent Works,* September 10–October 5.
Firehouse Art Center, Norman, Okla., *Clyde Connell: Recent Sculpture and Collages,*
    October 22–November 20.

Clyde Connell

1984
Delahunty Gallery, Dallas, *Clyde Connell: Recent Works*, May 22–June 23.

1985
Helen Lindhurst Fine Arts Gallery, University of Southern California, Los Angeles,
    National Women's Caucus for Art Sixth Annual Exhibition, February 12–16.
L.S.U. Union Art Gallery, Louisiana State University, Baton Rouge, *Clyde Connell:
    Recent Works*, February 22–March 14.
Southeastern Center for Contemporary Art, Winston-Salem, N.C., *Clyde Connell*, April
    6–May 26.
Louisiana State University Gallery, Shreveport, *Clyde Connell: Birthday Celebration*,
    September 4–30.
University of Southwestern Louisiana Art Museum, Lafayette, *Clyde Connell: Sculpture*,
    October 19–November 22.

1986
Arthur Roger Gallery, New Orleans, *Clyde Connell: Sculpture*, January 4–30.
Tyler (Tex.) Museum of Art, *Clyde Connell: A Fresh Look*, March 1–April 21.
Stoner Arts Center, Shreveport, La., *Clyde Connell*, November 1–30.

1987
Oscarsson Siegeltuch, New York, *Clyde Connell: Songs from Lake Bistineau*, April 1–
    May 2.

Selected Group Exhibitions

1974
Barnwell Garden and Art Center, Shreveport, La., *Contemporty Art Group*, June 16–
    July 16.

1975
Louisiana State University Library, Shreveport, *Clyde Connell, Sylvia Gallagher, Lucille
    Reed*, August 26–September 26.

1976
Meadows Museum of Art, Centenary College of Louisiana, Shreveport, *Juried Exhibition:
    Shreveport Artists Guild National*, October 22–November 19.

1977
Arkansas Art Center, Little Rock, *Twentieth Delta Annual*, October 14–November 13.

1979
Louisiana State University Library, Shreveport, *Clyde Connell, Betty Friedenberg*, April 3–
    May 10.

1980
Contemporary Arts Center, New Orleans, *Louisiana Major Works 1980*, January 12–
    February 24.

1981
Tyler (Tex.) Museum of Art, *Tenth Anniversary Show*, March 21–June 28.
Mississippi Museum of Art, Jackson, *Collage and Assemblage*, September 17–November 15,
    and tour to Tampa (Fla.) Museum, January 31–March 28, 1982; Alexandria (La.)
    Museum, Visual Art Center, May 1–June 5; Roanoke (Va.) Museum of Fine Arts,
    September 10–November 27; Tucson (Ariz.) Museum of Art, April 16–June 3, 1983;
    Hunter Museum of Art, Chattanooga, Tenn., November 13–January 9, 1984.

1982
Tibor de Nagy Gallery, New York, February 6–March 3.

1983
New Orleans Museum of Art, *1983 New Orleans Triennial*, April 8–May 22.
Art Museum of South Texas, Corpus Christi, *A Partial Look: The Atlantic Richfield
    Corporate Art Collection*, May 11–June 26.

University Museum, Southern Illinois University at Carbondale, *Louisiana Women in Contemporary Art,* October 28–November 23, and tour to Alexandria (La.) Museum, Visual Art Center, December 3–January 20, 1984; Meadows Museum of Art, Centenary College of Louisiana, Shreveport, La., January 26–February 19; Tilden-Foley Gallery, New Orleans, March 16–29.

1985
Barry Whistler Gallery, Dallas, *Inaugural Exhibition,* October 5–November 2.
D.W. Gallery, Dallas, *Tenth Anniversary Exhibition,* December 7–January 15, 1986.

1986
Everson Museum of Art, Syracuse, N.Y., *Other Gods,* February 15–March 30.
Neuberger Museum, State University of New York, Purchase, *Awards in the Visual Arts Five,* April 13–June 15, and tour to Columbus (Ohio) Museum of Art, September 14–October 18; Norton Gallery and School of Art, West Palm Beach, Fla., December 12–January 25, 1987.
Damon Brandt Gallery, New York, *Coded Messages: Calligraphy in Paintings and Drawings,* May 8–June 7.
University of South Florida, Tampa, *Southeast Sculptors: Comments on the Human Condition,* October 10–November 15.
Barry Whistler Gallery, Dallas, *Works on Paper,* November 1–29.

Selected Bibliography

Butera, Virginia Fabbri. "Group Show." *Arts Magazine* 56 (April 1982): 17.

Clyde Connell. Exhibition brochure. Alexandria, La.: Louisiana State University, 1973.

Clyde Connell: Recent Works. Exhibition brochure. Baton Rouge, La.: Louisiana State University, 1985.

Clyde Connell: Songs from Lake Bistineau. Exhibition brochure. New York: Oscarsson Siegeltuch, 1987. Statements by Lowery S. Sims, John Alexander, David Connelly, and James Surls.

Cohen, Ronny. "Clyde Connell: Oscarsson Siegeltuch." *Artforum* 26 (September 1987): 132.

Connelly, David. "Clyde Connell Exhibit: 'Altestil of a Serious Artist.'" *Shreveport Journal,* September 15, 1987, pp. 3C, 6C.

———. "Clyde Connell's Bound People." *Louisiana Life* (May–June 1987): 42–56.

———. "Connell Works Set for Hirshhorn." *Shreveport Journal,* April 29, 1987, p. 4C.

———. "Connell Returns to Tyler Art Museum." *Shreveport Journal,* March 11, 1986, p. 3B.

Curtis, Sandra J. "Texas Project." *Archives of American Art Journal* 21, no. 2 (1981): 30–31.

Harlan, Calvin. "Clyde Connell at the University Art Museum." *New Orleans Art Review* 5 (October–November 1985): 16–17.

Hill, Ed, and Suzanne Bloom. "Houston: Clyde Connell, Butler Gallery." *Artforum* 24 (December 1985): 97.

Kalil, Susie. "Clyde Connell . . ." *Artweek* 10 (November 10, 1979): 16.

Kutner, Janet. "Dallas: Seaworthy Sculpture." *Art News* 79 (Summer 1980) 207–10.

Moser, Charlotte. *An Exhibition of Works by Clyde Connell.* Exhibition brochure. Tyler, Tex.: Tyler Museum of Art, 1979.

———. "Houston: Clyde Connell." *Art in America* 61 (February 1980): 136–37.

Randolf, Lynn M. "Clyde Connell." *Woman's Art Journal* 6 (Fall 1985–Winter 1986): 30–34.

Surls, James. Statement in *Louisiana Women in Contemporary Art*. Exhibition catalog. Carbondale, Ill.: Southern Illinois University, 1983.

Vetrocq, Marcia E. "New Orleans, Clyde Connell at University Art Museum." *Art in America* 74 (May 1986): 167–68.

———. "Reviews, New Orleans." *Art in America* 71 (October 1983): 191–92.

Watson, Ronald. *Clyde Connell: Recent Paintings and Sculpture*. Exhibition brochure. Fort Worth: Texas Christian University, 1982.

Bruce Conner

Bruce Conner created his own memento mori in assemblages and collages of the late 1950s and the early 1960s. He often combined horror with terror in these pieces to convey the imminence and aura of death. But many of his works elicit compassion and pity, transcending morbidity with a concern for humanity.

While attending the Brooklyn Museum Art School in 1956, Conner became intrigued with metaphysics and a visionary world. After he moved to San Francisco in 1957 he began to make sculpture and collages out of perishable material, noting that ideas as well as forms were important. Unfortunately, much of this sculpture has disappeared or disintegrated. In 1964 Conner stopped producing sculpture and collages and devoted his time to drawings and short films, which had been parallel means of expression for years. Many of the drawings have complex elements that focus on the occult. Films such as *Cosmic Ray* and *A Movie* have become classics of the underground cinema.

Conner uses black frequently to convey the stench of decay and death. *Child,* 1959–60 (21), was originally an expression of the artist's objections to the death penalty, using the case of Caryl Chessman who was sentenced to die in the gas chamber. In the development of the assemblage, however, Conner changed his focus and created instead a moving indictment against inhumanity and cruelty. The charred and mutilated figure whose mouth is open in a stilled scream is an image drawn ready-made from the not-too-distant past—Hiroshima and the Nazi death camps come to mind. *Child* may also serve as a warning against future wars.

Ray Charles/Snakeskin, 1961 (25), is a tribute to the blind musician and his rhythm-and-blues. In a 1980 interview Conner said of the collage, "It's sort of a poetic statement to Ray Charles and to changing your skin."[1] (While shedding its skin, a snake cannot see because the skin covering its eyelids sloughs off along with that on the rest of its body.)

An untitled work from 1964 (27) could be a metaphor for the hopelessness of poverty. The collage is constructed of materials that are worn, torn, dirty, and a bit sordid. Linoleum is used throughout; some pieces are printed with floral patterns while other pieces imitate tile or wood grain. In the upper left-hand corner of the middle panel, risqué pictures from magazines are tucked under the linoleum. A small door that was cut into the surface of the middle panel is held shut by a Band-Aid. Fake flowers and a red paper heart decorate the middle panel, while a page of sheet music for "America: My Country 'tis of Thee" is attached to the left panel at the bottom. In this odd composition Conner arranged the pieces of linoleum to create barely noticeable forms, as though indicating hidden forces. For example, a figure can be discerned in the middle panel, while the profile of a hieratic figure can be read on the right panel.

Conner's work relates in many ways to medieval Italian painting, which exhorts the faithful by vividly portraying the agony of sinners in Hell, among other subjects. His twentieth-century warnings can be considered gruesome metaphors for the end of humanity. Yet it is death without benefit of an undertaker, for flesh is left to molder until cobwebs embrace the forms and a dull black patina covers all.

1. From the transcript of a tape in the San Francisco Museum of Modern Art Archives.

19
Odem, 1959
Paper, wax, glue, wire, and fabric on fiberboard; 20½ x 12 x 6 inches
Los Angeles County Museum of Art, anonymous gift

Bruce Conner

22
The Box, 1960
Wax figure, suitcase, tin cans, shredded nylon, etc., in wood box; 32¼ x 20⅜ x 35¼ inches
The Museum of Modern Art, New York, Larry Aldrich Foundation Fund

23
Medusa, 1960
Cardboard, hair, nylon, wax, and wood; 10¾ x 11 x 22¼ inches
Whitney Museum of American Art, New York, gift of the Howard and Jean Lipman Foundation, Inc.

24

Music, 1960
Film strip, wax, string, paint, Band-Aid, postage stamp, tape, string tags, and ink on music
sheet paper on cardboard with black velvet; 21⅝ x 11 x ½ inches
San Francisco Museum of Modern Art, gift of Mary Heath Keesling

25
Ray Charles/Snakeskin, 1961
Plastic, nylon, metal, paper, wood, paint, and snakeskin tissue on fiberboard; 25¾ x 18¾ inches
San Francisco Museum of Modern Art, gift of the Women's Board

26
Eagles Nest, 1962
Fabric, thread, cellophane, straw, paper, photographic etching, acrylic, and ink on fiberboard;
24½ x 22¼ x 1½ inches
San Francisco Museum of Modern Art, Albert M. Bender Collection

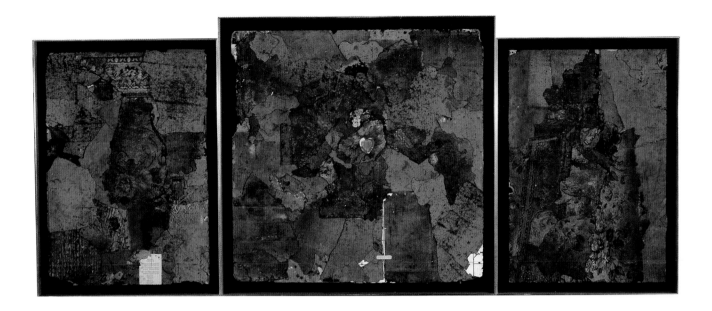

27
Untitled, 1964
Mixed media on fiberboard; three panels (left to right): 44⅛ x 31¼, 47¾ x 49½, 44¼ x 31 inches
Hirshhorn Museum and Sculpture Garden, Smithsonian Institution, Washington, D.C., museum purchase

Bruce Conner

Bruce Conner, 1973

Biography

Born Bruce Guldner Conner, November 18, 1933, in McPherson, Kansas. Education: Kansas City Art Institute, Missouri, and Wichita State University, Kansas, 1951–52; University of Nebraska, Lincoln, 1952–56, B.F.A. 1956; Brooklyn Museum Art School, 1956–57; University of Colorado, Boulder, 1957. Instructor: filmmaking, California College of Arts and Crafts, Oakland, 1965; life drawing, 1966–67, painting and sculpture, 1972, San Francisco Art Institute; U.C.L.A. Extension, 1973; painting, San Jose State University, 1974; filmmaking, San Francisco State University, 1976. Awards include: Ann Bremer Memorial Prize for Painting, 1958, and Neallie Sullivan Award, San Francisco Art Association, 1963; Ford Foundation Fellowship, 1964; William and Noma Copley Foundation Award, 1965; Tamarind Lithography Workshop Artist-Fellow, 1965; Visual Artists Fellowship, National Endowment for the Arts, 1973; Guggenheim Fellowship, 1975. Honorary D.F.A., San Francisco Art Institute, 1986. Lives and works in San Francisco.

Selected Solo Exhibitions

1956
Rienzi Gallery, New York.

1960
Alan Gallery, New York, *Bruce Conner*, January 18–February 6.

1961
Alan Gallery, New York, *Bruce Conner*, October 2–21.

1962
Ferus Gallery, Los Angeles, *Bruce Conner*, June 4–30.

1963
Wichita (Kans.) Art Museum, *Drawings by Bruce Conner*, February 10–March 3.
San Francisco Art Institute, *Bruce Conner*, November 4–22.

1964
Robert Fraser Gallery, London, *Bruce Conner*, December 1–January 9, 1965.

1965
Alan Gallery, New York, *Bruce Conner*, May 10–28.
Rose Art Museum, Brandeis University, Waltham, Mass., *Bruce Conner: Sculpture, Assemblages, Drawings, Films*, September 20–October 24.

1967
Institute of Contemporary Art, University of Pennsylvania, Philadelphia, *Bruce Conner: Sculpture, Assemblages, Collages, Drawings, Films,* November 29–December 31.

1974
Smith Andersen Gallery, Palo Alto, Calif., *Bruce Conner, Prints,* June 20–July 16.
M.H. de Young Museum, Fine Arts Museums of San Francisco, *Bruce Conner: Drawings 1955–1972,* October 4–January 5, 1975, and tour to Joslyn Art Museum, Omaha, Nebr., January 28–March 2; Wadsworth Atheneum, Hartford, Conn., April 1–May 11.

1975
Braunstein/Quay Gallery, San Francisco, *Angels: Bruce Conner,* October 7–November 1, and tour to Braunstein/Quay Gallery, New York, March 16–April 10, 1976.

1981
North Point Gallery, San Francisco, *Bruce Conner: Selected Works,* July 14–August 22.

1983
Fraenkel Gallery, San Francisco, *Angels: 1973–1975 Bruce Conner,* March 8–April 16.
Smith Andersen Gallery, Palo Alto, Calif., *Bruce Conner,* September 9–October 22.

1986
Fraenkel Gallery, San Francisco, *Bruce Conner: Selected Works (with Photographs 1959–1978),* September 24–October 25.

Selected Group Exhibitions

1958
San Francisco Art Association, San Francisco Museum of Art, *Seventy-Seventh Annual Painting and Sculpture Exhibition,* April 10–May 4.

1961
Krannert Art Museum, University of Illinois, Champaign, *Contemporary American Painting and Sculpture,* February 26–April 2.

1962
Whitney Museum of American Art, New York, *Fifty California Artists,* October 23–December 2, and tour to Walker Art Center, Minneapolis, February 17–March 17, 1963; Albright-Knox Art Gallery, Buffalo, N.Y., April 10–May 8; Des Moines (Iowa) Art Center, May 24–June 23.
Stanford University Art Gallery, Palo Alto, Calif., *Some Points of View,* October 30–November 20.

1964
Galleria George Lester, Rome, *Bruce Conner, James Gill,* June 3–23.
Whitney Museum of American Art, New York, *Annual Exhibition 1964: Contemporary American Sculpture,* December 9–January 31, 1965 (also included in 1979 Biennial).

1967
University Art Museum, University of California, Berkeley, *Funk,* April 18–May 29.
Los Angeles County Museum of Art, *American Sculpture of the Sixties,* April 28–June 25, and tour to Philadelphia Museum of Art, September 15–October 29.
Palazzo dei Congressi, San Marino, Italy, *Nuove Techniche d'Immagine, Sesta Biennale d'Arte,* July 15–September 30.

1968
Art Gallery, University of California, Irvine, *Assemblage in California,* October 15–November 24.

1969
Whitney Museum of American Art, New York, *Human Concern/Personal Torment,* October 14–November 30, and tour to University Art Museum, University of California, Berkeley, January 20–March 1, 1970.

1974

Dallas Museum of Fine Arts and Pollock Galleries, Southern Methodist University, Dallas, *Poets of the Cities: New York and San Francisco 1950–1965,* November 20–December 29, and tour to San Francisco Museum of Modern Art, January 31–March 23, 1975; Wadsworth Atheneum, Hartford, Conn., April 23–June 1.

1975

Mount Holyoke College, South Hadley, Mass., *Art As a Muscular Principle/Ten Artists and San Francisco 1950–1965,* February 28–March 20.

1976

Newport Harbor Art Museum, Newport Beach, Calif., *The Last Time I Saw Ferus 1957–1966,* March 7–April 17.

San Francisco Museum of Modern Art, *Painting and Sculpture in California: The Modern Era,* September 3–November 21, and tour to National Collection of Fine Arts, Washington, D.C., May 20–September 11, 1977.

1977

Musée National d'Art Moderne, Paris, *Paris-New York,* June 1–September 19.

1984

Museum of Modern Art, New York, *Primitivism in Twentieth Century Art,* September 27–January 15, 1985, and tour to Detroit Institute of Arts, February 27–May 19; Dallas Museum of Art, June 23–September 1.

1987

University Art Museum, University of California, Berkeley, *Made in USA: An Americanization in Modern Art, the Fifties and Sixties,* April 4–June 21, and tour to Nelson-Atkins Museum of Art, Kansas City, Mo., July 25–September 6; Virginia Museum of Fine Arts, Richmond, October 7–December 7.

Selected Bibliography

Anderson, Laurie. "Reviews and Previews." *Art News* 71 (November 1972): 89.

Ashton, Dore. "Art." *Arts and Architecture* 77 (March 1960): 35.

Berkson, William. "Bruce Conner." *Arts Magazine* 39 (September–October 1965): 64.

Bruce Conner: Sculpture, Assemblages, Drawings, Films. Exhibiton catalog. Waltham, Mass.: Rose Art Museum, Brandeis University, 1965. Text by Thomas H. Garver.

Bruce Conner. Exhibition brochure. Palo Alto: Smith Andersen Gallery, 1983. Text by Sam Francis.

Bruce Conner: Drawings 1955–1972. Exhibition catalog. San Francisco: Fine Arts Museums of San Fancisco, 1974. Text by Thomas H. Garver.

Bruce Conner Prints. Exhibition catalog. Palo Alto, Calif.: Smith Andersen Gallery, 1974. Text by Peter Selz.

Bruce Conner: Sculpture, Assemblages, Collages, Drawings, Films. Exhibition catalog. Philadelphia: Institute of Contemporary Art, 1967. Texts by Joan C. Siegfried and Stephen S. Prokopoff.

Burr, James. "London Galleries Artless Art." *Apollo* 80 (December 1964): 518–20.

Campbell, Lawrence. "Bruce Conner." *Art News* 59 (March 1960): 62.

Chipp, Herschel B. "San Francisco." *Art News* 59 (February 1961): 54.

Cook, Scott. "Uncanny Resurrections of 'America Is Waiting.'" *Artforum* 20 (January 1982): 34–37.

Flanagan Ann. "Bruce Conner's Cinematic Drawings." *Artweek* 5 (November 9, 1974): 1, 16.

Frank, Peter. "Bruce Conner." *Art News* 75 (May 1976): 34.

Fuller, Mary. "San Francisco Sculptors." *Art in America* 52 (June 1964): 52–59.

Garver, Thomas H. "Bruce Conner Makes a Sandwich." *Artforum* 6 (September 1967): 51–55.

Greene, Merril. "Bruce Conner," in *Art As a Muscular Principle/ Ten Artists and San Francisco*. Exhibition catalog. South Hadley, Mass.: Mount Holyoke College, 1975, pp. 32–39.

Leider, Philip. "Bruce Conner: A New Sensibility." *Artforum* 1 (November–December 1962): 30–31. Excerpt reprinted in *Assemblage in California*. Exhibition catalog. Irvine: University of California, 1968, p. 32.

McClure, Michael. *Bruce Conner/Michael McClure*. San Francisco: Dave Haselwood, 1966. (Poems by Michael McClure, drawings by Bruce Conner).

MacDonald, Scott. "I Don't Go to the Movies Anymore: An Interview with Bruce Conner." *Afterimage* 10 (Summer 1982): 20–23.

Moritz, William, and Beverly O'Neill. "Fallout: Some Notes on the Films of Bruce Conner." *Film Quarterly* 32 (Summer 1978): 36–42.

Mosen, David. "Report." *Film Quarterly* 19 (Spring 1966): 54–56.

Reveaux, Anthony. *Bruce Conner*. St. Paul, Minn.: Film in the Cities, 1981.

"Sculpture Savonarola in Nylon Skeins." *Time* 91 (January 5, 1968): 50.

Selz, Peter. "The Artist as Dactylographer." *Art in America* 62 (July–August 1974): 98–99.

———. "Recent Series by Bruce Conner." *Arts Magazine* 58 (May 1984): 102–3.

Solnit, Rebecca. "Intrepid Chameleon." *Artweek* 17 (March 15, 1986): 11.

Tarshis, Jerome. "Bruce Conner is not 'Bruce Conner.'" *Art News* 76 (January 1977): 80–87.

Tuchman, Mitch. "Bruce Conner Interviewed by Mitch Tuchman." *Film Comment* 17 (September–October 1981): 73–76.

Öyvind Fahlström

Öyvind Fahlström's varied works wrap personal concerns in recognizable symbols and images to communicate the materialism, violence, and greed that he felt was inhibiting world peace and progress. In his drawings, paintings, and constructions he used figures and signs to refer to these indecencies directly, or by allusion. His works were meant to be read as well as be looked at, although their meanings are often more intuitive than specific. References to big business, government agencies, and politics appear throughout his work. Although his comments were often presented in a playful manner, he wanted his work to be taken seriously.

Falhström was an artist, poet, playwright, and filmmaker. His interests were encyclopedic, ranging from pre-Columbian codices to contemporary economics, and he could read at least five languages. Before settling in the United States in 1961, he had lived in Brazil and Sweden, where he studied archeology and art history at Stockholm University. He had his first solo exhibition at a gallery in Florence, Italy, in 1952. In 1961 he received an award from the Sweden-America Foundation to study in the United States. Fahlström's political orientation was Socialist/Marxist, which reinforced his opinions about the international establishment.

Many of his early paintings contain elements based on comic strips that he translated into enigmatic nonfigurative forms. Fahlström's cartoon style relates to the humorous absurdities of "Krazy Kat" or the wide-eyed simplicity of "Orphan Annie," not to the heroic and glamorous cartoon stereotypes ("Terry and the Pirates," for example) favored by Pop artists. His figures were often combined with recognizable caricatures of such public figures as Richard Nixon, Henry Kissinger, and Mao Zedong. In later works Fahlström often attached these images to magnets so that viewers could move them at will on metal game boards in order to create, and recreate, relationships. In this way viewers could become physically and intellectually involved in his schema, which expressed how the world was being manipulated by the powerful.

The title for *Sitting . . . ,* 1962 (28), is a shortened version of *Sitting Like Pat with a Bat on Her Hat*—a nonsense rhyme the artist composed about a funny hat Claes Oldenburg's first wife, Pat, wore at a party. The words appear in the painting, right of center. The title also refers to the "Batman" comics Fahlström was using in his work (see the lower left of the painting).[1] The format and forms are similar to those of a comic book page, but this painting is not organized in a comic book's usual sequential arrangement of frames. White lines isolate discontinuous segments that, like comic strips, express space and time—the action takes place over time and often changes location. Some of the forms are recognizable, such as an elephant's foot or a periscope, but they serve only to deepen the mystery as they lead us through the picture. The viewer can begin to understand, or read, the picture as an assembly of obscure situations involving flaming muzzles, explosions, smoke, and water that defy verbal explanation.

The frames and narration in *Performing K.K. No. 2 (Sunday Edition)*, 1963–64 (29), are close to the usual comic strip format. George Herriman's "Krazy Kat" (syndicated in various newspapers across the country from 1910 to 1944) told the fanciful tale of Ofissa Pup, a guardian of law and order, and his battles with the cynical trouble-making Ignatz Mouse and Krazy Kat, who maintained a love-hate relationship with the officer. In Fahlström's version, words have a primary function, as they do in Herriman's original. It is all acted out in a flat simple world with little architecture and vegetation. Fahlström put the main characters in their usual ridiculous confrontation but also included some enigmatic forms that cannot be read as specific objects but that intensify the visual movement of the scenes. Ofissa Pup stood for the establishment; the artist's sympathy lay with the "revolutionary" mouse who represented the underprivileged. The unreality and immorality of the comic strip world fascinated Fahlström because he thought it mirrored the absurd modes of perception of many people in the real world. By removing the popular comic strip from its amusing simplistic context and putting it into a more serious arena, the artist hoped to focus the viewer's attention on attitudes about politics.

The *Notes for Dr. Schweitzer's Last Mission A and B*, 1966 (31, 32), are sheets filled with sketches of the forms that appear in a large installation consisting of eight painted metal boxes, ten cutout boards, and fifty magnetic iron and plastic cutouts that were affixed to the walls or hung by nylon threads from the walls and ceiling. Dr. Schweitzer's mission had been to aid the poor and disadvantaged people of the world. Fahlström put the doctor among a welter of symbols and forms that represent the pain and destruction in many parts of the world. Is it then Schweitzer's last mission to rid the world of this malaise?

The structure of Öyvind Fahlström's work is a metaphor for the world and a means of perceiving its faults. He often drew on elements from the world around him to express a disordered and disintegrating society. Although he was friendly with many of the Pop artists, Fahlström's work cannot be considered part of their influential style. He stood apart, with his own deep convictions about the contemporary culture that his friends used for inspiration.

---

1. Suzi Gablik, "Fahlström: A Place for Everything," *Art News* 65 (Summer 1966): 62.

28
Sitting . . ., 1962
Tempera on paper mounted on canvas; 62⅝ x 79⅛ inches
Moderna Museet, Stockholm

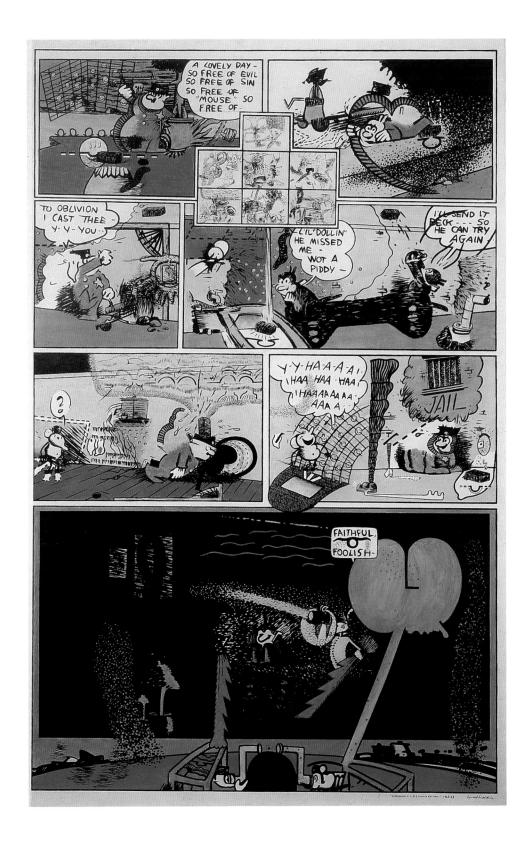

29
Performing K.K. No. 2 (Sunday Edition), 1963–64
Tempera on paper mounted on canvas; 52 x 34 inches
Mr. and Mrs. S.I. Newhouse, Jr., New York

30
Sitting . . . Blocks, 1965–66
Tempera on vinyl and wood; ten blocks, each 15 x 15 x 15 inches
Sharon Avery-Fahlström, courtesy Arnold Herstand and Company, New York

31
Notes for Dr. Schweitzer's Last Mission A, 1966
Tempera and acrylic on paper; 29½ x 19½ inches
Courtesy Sidney Janis Gallery, New York

32
Notes for Dr. Schweitzer's Last Mission B, 1966
Tempera and ink on paper; 29½ x 19½ inches
Courtesy Sidney Janis Gallery, New York

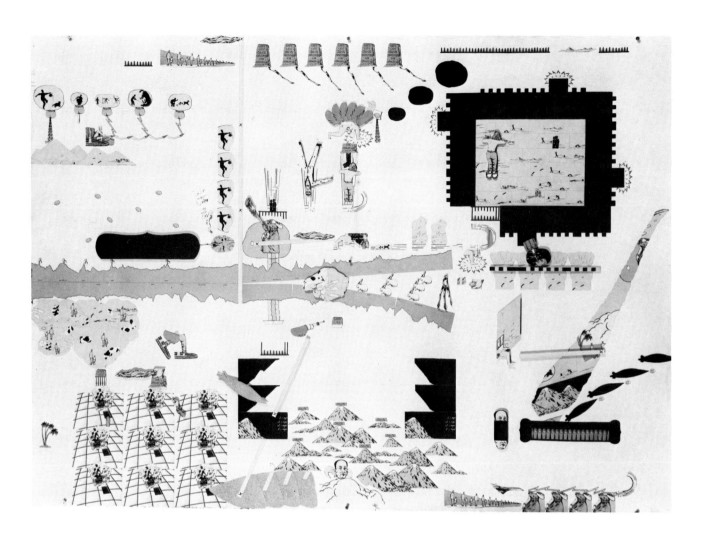

33
Eddie (Sylvie's Brother) in the Desert (Collage), 1966
Fifteen movable serigraphed paper cutouts over serigraphed cutouts pasted on painted wood;
35¼ x 50¼ inches
The Museum of Modern Art, New York, Sidney and Harriet Janis Collection

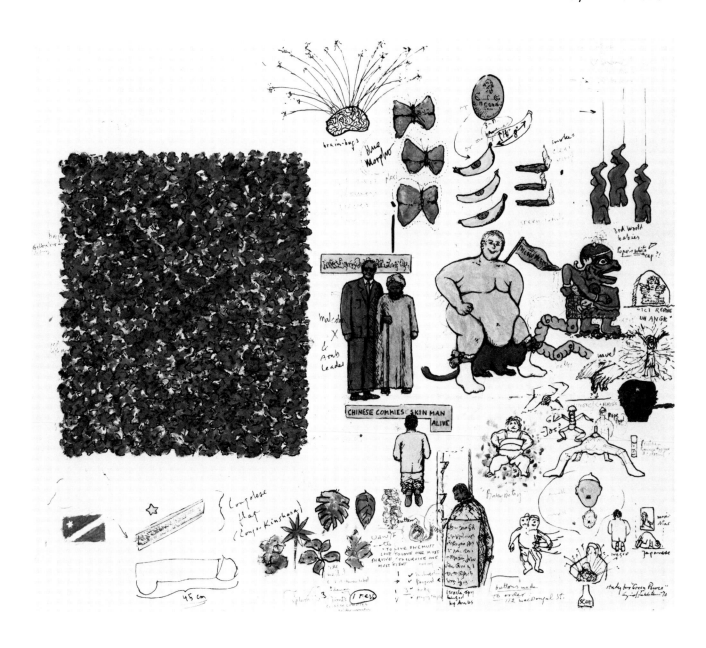

34
Study for "Green Power," 1970
Tempera and ink on paper; 14 x 16⁹⁄₁₆ inches
Solomon R. Guggenheim Museum, New York

35
Notes 5 (Wrestlers), 1971
Ink and acrylic on paper; 16⁹⁄₁₆ x 14 inches
Courtesy Sidney Janis Gallery, New York

Öyvind Fahlström, 1976

Biography

Born Öyvind Axel Christian Fahlström, December 28, 1928, in São Paulo, Brazil; became a Brazilian citizen. Moved to Sweden, 1939; became a Swedish citizen, 1947. Education: University of Stockholm, 1949–52. Theater critic and journalist, Stockholm, 1950–55. Received Sweden-America Foundation Award and moved to New York, 1961. Awards include: Painting Prize, *V Bienal de São Paulo,* 1959; Prize of the National Museum of Western Art, *Ninth International Biennial Exhibition of Prints in Tokyo 1974,* Tokyo, 1974. Died November 8, 1976, in Stockholm.

Selected Solo Exhibitions

1952
Galleria Numero, Florence.

1959
Galerie Daniel Cordier, Paris, *Öyvind Fahlström,* February 19–March 15.
Galerie Blanche, Stockholm, *Öyvind Fahlström,* April.

1962
Galerie Daniel Cordier, Paris, *Öyvind Fahlström,* December 6–January 12, 1963.

1964
Cordier and Eckstrom, New York. *Öyvind Fahlström,* October 4–29.

1967
Sidney Janis Gallery, New York, *Fahlström,* February 1–25.

1969
Sidney Janis Gallery, New York, *New Works by Öyvind Fahlström,* March 5–29.
Galerie Zwirner, Cologne, *Öyvind Fahlström,* October.

1971
Sidney Janis Gallery, New York, *Fahlström,* March 17–April 10.

1973
Sidney Janis Gallery, New York, *Exhibition of New Work by Öyvind Fahlström,* April 4–28.

1974
Galerie Buchholz, Munich, *Fahlström,* April 9–June 5.

1976
Sidney Janis Gallery, New York, *Exhibition of New Work by Öyvind Fahlström,* March 18–
 April 10.

1977
Galerie Baudoin Lebon, Paris, *Öyvind Fahlström,* January 24–February 24.

1979
Moderna Museet, Stockholm, *Öyvind Fahlström,* October 13–December 9.

1982
Sidney Janis, New York, *Öyvind Fahlström, 1928–1976,* January 7–30.
Solomon R. Guggenheim Museum, New York, *Öyvind Fahlström,* September 14–
 November 7.

1984
Arnold Herstand, New York, *Öyvind Fahlström,* March 15–April 10.

1987
Arnold Herstand, New York, *Öyvind Fahlström,* April 9–May 16.

Selected Group Exhibitions

1958
Carnegie Institute, Department of Fine Arts, Pittsburgh, *The 1958 Pittsburgh Bicentennial
 International Exhibition of Contemporary Painting and Sculpture,* December 5–February 8,
 1959.

1959
Museu de Arte Moderna, São Paulo, *V Bienal de São Paulo,* September 21–December 31.

1962
Sidney Janis Gallery, New York, *New Realists,* October 31–December 1.

1964
Venice, *XXXII Biennale Internazionale d'Arte Venezia,* June–October (also included in 1966,
 1972 Biennales).
Museum des 20. Jahrhunderts, Vienna, *Pop etc.,* September 19–October 31.

1966
Sidney Janis Gallery, New York, *Erotic Art,* October 3–29.

1967
Palazzo dei Congressi, San Marino, Italy, *Nuove Techniche d'Immagine, Sesta Biennale
 d'Arte,* July 15–September 30.
Museum of Contemporary Art, Chicago, *Pictures to Be Read/Poetry to Be Seen,* October
 24–December 3.
Sidney Janis Gallery, New York, *Homage to Marilyn Monroe,* December 6–30.

1968
Musée des Arts Décoratifs, Paris, *Pentacle, Olle Baertling, Öyvind Fahlström, . . . ,*
 January 18–March 31.
Museum Fridericianum, Orangerie im Auepark, Kassel, West Germany, *4. Documenta,*
 June 27–October 6.

1969
Los Angeles County Museum of Art, *Art and Technology,* May 11–August 29.
Hayward Gallery, London, *Pop Art Redefined,* July 9–September 3.
Institute of Contemporary Art, University of Pennsylvania, Philadelphia, *The Spirit of the
 Comics,* October 1–November 9.

1970
Sidney Janis Gallery, New York, *String and Rope,* January 7–31.
Institute of Contemporary Art, University of Pennsylvania, Philadelphia, *Against Order:*

Chance and Art, November 14–December 22.
Sidney Janis Gallery, New York, *Seven Artists: New Work,* December 4–31.

1972
National Museum of Modern Art, Tokyo, *Swedish Art 1972,* April 8–May 21, and tour to National Museum of Modern Art, Kyoto, May 27–June 18.

1974
National Museum of Modern Art, Tokyo, *Ninth International Biennial Exhibition of Prints in Tokyo 1974,* November 18–January 15, 1975, and tour to National Museum of Modern Art, Kyoto, January 21–March 2.

1976
Museum of Modern Art, New York, *Drawing Now 1955–1975,* January 21–March 9.

1987
Institute of Contemporary Art, London, *Comic Iconoclasm,* June–September, and tour to Douglas Hyde Gallery, Dublin, October–November; Cornerhouse Gallery, Manchester, January–February 1988.

Bibliography

Adrian, Dennis. "Fahlström: Three Faces of Öyv." *Artforum* 5 (April 1967): 47–48.

Ashton, Dore. "Art—with Irony." *Studio International* 173 (January 1967): 40–43.

Crichton, Fenella. "Paris Letter." *Art International* 21 (March–April 1977): 56–59.

Ekbom, Torstem. "Öyvind Fahlström: Models of Shattered Reality." *Art International* 10 (Summer 1966): 40–56.

Fahlström, Öyvind. "A Game of Character." *Art and Literature* 3 (Autumn–Winter 1964): 220–26.

———. "Le jeux de monopoly." *Opus International* 29–30 (December 1971): 63–64.

———. "Object-making." *Studio International* 172 (December 1966): 328;-29.

Fahlström. Exhibition catalog. New York: Sidney Janis Gallery, 1971.

Fahlström. Exhibition catalog. Munich: Galerie Buchholz, 1974. Text by K. Liebig.

Fahlström. Milan: Multhipla Edizione, 1976. Text by Lazlo Glozer.

Gablik, Suzi. "Fahlström: A Place for Everything." *Art News* 65 (Summer 1966): 38–41, 61–64.

Gassiot-Talabot, Gerald. "Le grand jeu d'Öyvind Fahlström." *Opus International* 4 (December 1967): 78–79.

Hulten, Karl G. "Öyvind Fahlström." *Quadrum* 8 (1960): 150–51.

Judd, Donald. "Öyvind Fahlström." *Arts Magazine* 38 (March 1964): 65–66.

Kuspit, Donald B. "Öyvind Fahlstöm's Political Puzzles." *Art in America* 70 (April 1982): 106–11.

Linker, Kate. "Öyvind Fahlström's Political Gamesmanship." *Artforum* 17 (October 1978): 64–70.

Livingston, Jane. "Öyvind Fahlström," in *A Report on the Art and Technology Program of the Los Angeles County Museum of Art.* Los Angeles: Los Angeles County Museum of Art, 1971, pp. 102–13.

Öyvind Fahlström. Exhibition brochure. Paris: Galerie Daniel Cordier, 1962. Text by Robert Rauschenberg.

Öyvind Fahlström. Exhibition catalog. Stockholm: Moderna Museet, 1979. Texts by Öyvind Fahlström, Ilmar Laaban, Robert Rauschenberg, Pontus Hulten, et al.

Öyvind Fahlström. Exhibition catalog. New York: Solomon R. Guggenheim Museum, 1982. Texts by Öyvind Fahlström, Olle Granath, Ilmar Laaban, et al.

Öyvind Fahlström. Exhibition catalog. New York: Arnold Herstand, 1984. Text by Öyvind Fahlström.

Öyvind Fahlström. Exhibition catalog. New York: Arnold Herstand, 1987. Text by Lawrence Alloway.

Rauschenberg, Robert. "Öyvind Fahlström." *Art and Literature* 3 (Autumn–Winter 1964): 219.

Robert Helm

Robert Helm's cryptic shadowboxes and paintings with wood elements function for the artist as reliquaries evoking memories of experiences that had obsessed him. His art is generated by a need to bring those moments back to life in compositions that replicate the intensity of the feeling he experienced.

First trained as a painter, Helm apprenticed himself to a steel engraver after being attracted by the quality of the decoration he saw on a handmade English saddle. He has no interest in craftsmanship for its own sake. Instead, he employs skills usually associated with wood and leather crafts to create exquisitely constructed and carved wood shadowboxes as well as paintings, which include wood as an enigmatic formal element.

Wood has always been important to Helm's work. In the 1970s his efforts consisted almost entirely of carved wood boxes that contained esoteric objects with mysterious overtones. For example, he used porcupine quills in an untitled work from 1975 (37), and deer horn and leather in *For a Time We Were All Silent and Moody Even in the Security of the House,* 1966–77 (38). Into the frame of the first-mentioned work, he also hammered nails to spell out words, each of which is decipherable only when viewed at a certain angle. Later Helm combined wood with painted images in two-dimensional compositions. When wood is part of a painting, he paints it with thin glazes to create the illusion of form and shadow. One of his main objectives is to marry the painted and wood surfaces in order to eliminate the visually disruptive "tacked on" appearance of some collages. Each of Helm's works challenges his technical knowledge and skill, his ability successfully to integrate the pieces of wood with thin layers of paint.

Referring to the scenes and objects that attract his attention, Helm has said: "The locations I return to are mundane enough, streets, a row of trees, a certain building. The compulsion to return, to take another look, seems to be common to most people. If these locations are curiously charged with meaning it is probable, at such places, you can meet with yourself going backwards."[1] When he finds places or things that obsess him (are "charged with meaning") and that he wishes to record in his art, he changes their appearance to create images that subtly express his emotions during the original experience. The romantic notion of capturing a fleeting moment plays an important role in Helm's work.

Helm notes that "art at its best should be a catalyst for meaning and that the meaning should not be limited."[2] Wanting the viewer to keep an open mind, he has no desire to interpret his works, and he does not care whether viewers understand what he is trying to describe. His works affect each viewer differently, depending on the experience and personality of the individual.

The title, *He Was Surprised That She Referred to Her Veiled Attempt As an Accomplished Fact,* 1979 (39), does not relate to the image. Even by itself the title is obscure, yet it does convey a sense of disagreement between two people about meaning. According to the artist, the image refers to his feeling about the absurdity of death. There is subtle humor in Death's attempt to knock a little twig off a tree in light of the grim reaper's more odious duties. The bullet-tipped object in Death's hands is held under tension by a leather thong. Like all organic materials, the leather will decompose and thus release the blade that will in turn slice the twig in its path, creating a new version of the work that Helm will probably not live to see. He has built such time changes into many of his boxes.

Shadows in *1983* (42) imply light coming from both left and right. The date is engraved on what appears to be a slab of marble. The improbable flame, the choppy water, and the mountains and hills in the background refer to three basic elements: fire, water, and earth.

Traveling on trains offers Helm a view not seen from the streets. The stimulus for *Dining Car,* 1984 (45), was a scene from one of his trips. As his train passed a dining car pulled off on a siding somewhere in Germany, Helm looked out his window and saw the dining car's well-polished wood gleaming in what appeared to be a soft amber light. Along with the sudden pleasurable impact of what he had just seen, Helm realized that he would never again experience that same scene. In order to convey the various sensations he had just experienced, Helm committed to memory not the interior's physical details but emotions the scene summoned up in him. The bird with marble-like feathers is caught in flight, suggesting that time is standing still.

Helm's materials often have exotic histories. Probably as luxurious as the wood he saw in the original dining car scene, the rosewood in *Dining Car* came from the interior of the schooner *Equator,* which was decaying in a dry dock on the Washington State coast. Robert Louis Stevenson had used this boat to sail to the South Seas when he was dying of tuberculosis.

Splitting Moon, 1987 (46), combines various images into an improbable scene. A coffin-like box with a bird perched on one side floats in calm water under a cloudy sky. A mirror appears to reflect the interior of the box, but a closer look reveals an image similar to the exterior of the box. The moon visible in the mirror seems to be positioned behind the viewer's shoulder, but three other moon forms are reflected in the water.

Memories and obsessions, the passage of time, and the power of the mind to give painted and constructed images a life of their own are the focus of Helm's work. Interpretations of his works may vary, but experiencing them is enriching and basic.

1. Helm in Bruce Guenther, *Fifty Northwest Artists: A Critical Selection of Painters and Sculptors Working in the Pacific Northwest* (San Francisco: Chronicle Books, 1983), 48–49.

2. From a 1987 interview with the author.

36
The Race, 1968–69
Wood, leather, and rocks; two framed pieces, each 17¼ x 17¼ x 2¾ inches
Ed and Nancy Kienholz, Hope, Idaho

37
Untitled, 1975
Leather, wood, and porcupine quills; 35¼ x 35¼ x 3¼ inches
Ed and Nancy Kienholz, Hope, Idaho

38
For a Time We Were All Silent and Moody, Even in the Security of the House, 1966–77
Walnut, mirror, leather, and deer horn; 26 x 29⅜ x 3⅝ inches
Nicholas Wilder, New York

39
He Was Surprised That She Referred to Her Veiled Attempt As an Accomplished Fact, 1979
Bark, wood, metal, and leather; 35 x 42 x 3¼ inches
Courtesy Edward Thorp Gallery, New York

40
*The Next Year, One Very Hot Sunday, All the Details of the Memorable Conversation Suddenly
Came Back to Him,* 1980
Wood and metal; 31⅛ x 31⅛ x 3½ inches
Mr. and Mrs. Klaus Groenke, Berlin

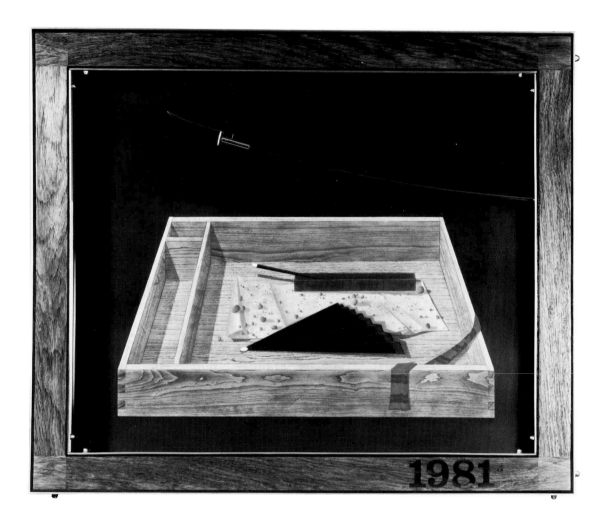

41
She Stared, Now at Her Gloved Hand, Now at the Unfamiliar Room, 1981
Wood and metal; 29½ x 35⅝ x 3 inches
Mr. and Mrs. Klaus Groenke, Berlin

42
1983, 1983
Oil on board with wood inlay; 29 x 23¼ x 1¼ inches
Wendy and Alan Hart, Topanga, California

43
Coral Tree, 1983
Oil on board with wood inlay; 27½ x 20⅝ inches
Hirshhorn Museum and Sculpture Garden, Smithsonian Institution, Washington, D.C., gift
of the Leonard C. Yaseen Foundation

44
Garden, 1983
Oil on board with wood inlay; 30 x 23¼ x 1½ inches
Stephen S. Alpert, Waltham, Massachusetts

45
Dining Car, 1984
Oil on board with wood inlay, brass, and leather; 31¾ x 23½ x 1¼ inches
Martin Sklar, New York

46
Splitting Moon, 1987
Oil on board with wood inlay, 39¼ x 60 inches
Courtesy Edward Thorp Gallery, New York

Robert Helm

Robert Helm, 1982

Biography

Born Robert Helm, January 13, 1943, in Wallace, Idaho. Education: Washington State University, Pullman, B.A., 1967, M.F.A., 1969. Instructor: University of Colorado, Boulder, 1969–71; Washington State University, 1971–present. Awards include: Deutscher Akademischer Austauschdienst Fellowship, 1978. Lives and works in Pullman, Washington.

Selected Solo Exhibitions

1970
Wesleyan University, Lincoln, Nebr., *Robert Helm,* March 1–20.

1974
Fine Arts Gallery, Washington State University, Pullman, *Robert Helm,* February 6–25.

1976
Nicholas Wilder Gallery, Los Angeles, *Robert Helm: Sculpture 1967–1976,* April 20–May 8.

1977
Nicholas Wilder Gallery, Los Angeles, *Robert Helm: New Work,* January 10–February 4.
Faith and Charity in Hope Gallery, Hope, Idaho, *Robert Helm,* July.

1982
Galerie Redmann, Berlin, *Robert Helm,* May 6–June 5.

1983
Seattle Art Museum, *Documents Northwest: The Poncho Series, Robert Helm,* December 8–
    January 8, 1984.

1984
Contemporary Arts Museum, Houston, Tex., *Robert Helm: Recent Work,* January 28–
    March 11.
L.A. Louver, Venice, Calif., *Robert Helm,* May 1–26.

1987
Edward Thorp Gallery, New York, *Robert Helm,* January 31–February 28.

Selected Group Exhibitions

1975
Missoula (Mont.) Museum of the Arts, *Concepts and Executions of Eight Sculptors,*
September 2–October 24.

1977
Musée d'Art Moderne de la Ville de Paris, *Dixième Biennale de Paris,* September 17–
November 1.
Museum of Art, Washington State University, Pullman, *Two Decades 1957–1977: Sculpture
from American Northwest Collections,* October 7–November 18.

1980
Middendorf/Lane Gallery, Washington, D.C., *Tableaux: An American Selection,* September
2–October 11.

1984
Crocker Art Museum, Sacramento, Calif., *Contemporary American Wood Sculpture,*
November 3–January 5, 1985, and Art Museum Association of America tour to
University of Arizona, Tucson, March 1–30; Sunrise Museum, Charleston, W. Va.,
May 17–August 18; Visual Arts Center, Florida International University, Miami,
October 15–November 30; Huntsville (Ala.) Museum of Art, January 5–February 16,
1986; Anchorage (Alaska) Historical and Fine Arts Museum, March 16–April 27.

1986
Phoenix Art Museum, *New Narrative Painting,* March 14–April 27. Neuberger Museum,
State University of New York, Purchase, *Awards in the Visual Arts Five,* April 13–
June 15, and tour to Columbus (Ohio) Museum of Art, September 14–October 18;
Norton Gallery and School of Art, West Palm Beach, Fla., December 12–January 25,
1987.
University Art Gallery, California State University Dominguez Hills, Carson, *Miracles and
Mysteries,* October 9–November 7.

1987
Whitney Museum of American Art, New York, *1987 Biennial Exhibition,* April 10–July 5
and March 31–June 28.

Selected Bibliography

Brenson, Michael. "Robert Helm," *New York Times,* February 6, 1987, p. C23.

Glowen, Ron. "Robert Helm at the Seattle Art Museum." *Art in America* 72 (May 1984):
181.

———. "Unanswered Riddles: Robert Helm." *Artweek* 14 (December 24, 1983): 6.

Helm, Robert. Statement in Bruce Guenther. *Fifty Northwest Artists: A Critical Selection of
Painters and Sculptors Working in the Pacific Northwest.* San Francisco: Chronicle Books,
1983, pp. 48–49.

Ivory, James. "In the American Grain." *Artforum* 23 (November 1984): 74–76.

Menzies, Neal. "Romantic Uses of Wood." *Artweek* 15 (May 19, 1984): 3.

Muchnic, Suzanne. "Robert Helm's Containers for Materials and Ideas." *Artweek* 9
(January 28, 1978): 3.

Perlmutter, Elizabeth. "Master Drawings, Voluptuous Boxes." *Art News* 75 (September
1976): 75–76.

Robert Helm. Exhibition catalog. Hope, Idaho: Faith and Charity in Hope Gallery, 1977.

Robert Helm. Exhibition catalog. Berlin: Galerie und Junsthandel, Inh. Hans Redmann,
1982.

Wallach, Amei. "Robert Helm. . . ." *New York Newsday Weekend*, February 6, 1967, pp. 26–27.

Wilson, William. "Robert Helm" in *Dixième Biennale de Paris*. Exhibition catalog. Paris: Musée d'Art Moderne de la Ville de Paris, 1977, pp. 152–53.

Wortz, Melinda. "Los Angeles, Love Poems." *Art News* 77 (April 1978): 120–26.

Yau, John. "Robert Helm: Edward Thorp Gallery." *Artforum* (Summer 1987): 119.

Alfred Jensen

Alfred Jensen used diagrams incorporating grids, forms, and colors that were often encoded with symbols and organized in arcane systems. Concentrated study sometimes reveals his rationales, but the paintings and drawings are the most important part of his legacy. Their intricate beauty overshadows the need to know whether the systems can be proven scientifically correct. Through color and mathematics Jensen portrayed ancient Greek temple plans and Mayan architecture as well as scientific formulas.

Jensen had been a cabin boy, a chicken farmer, and a cowboy before he received a scholarship to attend the San Diego Fine Arts School in 1924. The following year he worked on a German boat to get across the Atlantic so he could attend Hans Hofmann's school in Munich. In 1927 he felt restricted by Hofmann's teaching and left the school. Saidie Adler May, a wealthy art collector who was also one of Hofmann's students, became Jensen's patron, which allowed him to continue his studies. In 1951 he settled in New York City and began exhibiting and receiving favorable critical attention. Because his work is multifaceted and hard to understand, Jensen was largely ignored by the art world. His exhibition of nine paintings at the Guggenheim in 1961 was his first solo museum exhibition in this country.

He was intrigued by Goethe's color theories, which eschewed scientific theory based on Isaac Newton's observations about color in favor of more romantic ideas. Jensen often reinterpreted traditionally accepted concepts that he felt were conventionally misunderstood, for example, the Pythagorean theorem, in order to reveal their hidden meanings.

The dominating image in *My Oneness, a Universe of Colours,* 1957 (47), is a circle of concentric rings of color. The circle symbolizes women while the edges of the canvas symbolize men. In this painting Jensen expressed the eternal relationship (men and women) and his love of color, juxtaposing a reminder of mortality in a sentence from the death scene in Shakespeare's *King Lear.* "So we'll live and pray and sing and tell old tales and laugh at gilded butterflies." Below and on the left and right sides of the circle are written "Self Identity" and "Self Integration," self-evident concepts. At the bottom is a quote from Nathanael West: "No repeated group of words would fit their rhythm and no scale would give them meaning."[1]

The subject for *Entoptic Color,* 1959 (48), comes directly from a supplement to Goethe's book on color theory. In it he outlines an experiment about the effects of daylight reflected off black-backed glass panes in certain positions. Jensen's painting on the subject combines, symbolically, the results at various stages of Goethe's experiment.

The diptych *Heaven and Earth, The Ten Thousand Things,* 1972 (52), is composed of squares, rectangles, and triangles defined by about ten thousand dots of paint that look like tufts in a tapestry or units of time to measure the eye's cadence across the canvas. Allan Kaprow, who gained fame through his "happenings" during the 1960s, once remarked: "Spatial extension in any direction is exactly measured by giving the eyeballs a periodic movement, square by square, movement after movement."[2] A large square, built from four smaller squares that are the same size, dominates each panel. The geometric elements are so carefully placed and interlocked that relationships appear and disappear as the viewer's focus changes. The subject matter can be interpreted in several different ways, yet this work can be approached simply as a well-balanced, well-composed work of art.

Jensen did not attempt to replicate or define the world as most people see it, nor did he approach his art with the formalism of an abstract composition. Instead, he devised systems and diagrams that conveyed the meanings, orders, and dualities of things around him. His paintings cannot be read and understood quickly, although they can be read on many levels and be appreciated both visually and conceptually.

1. See Linda L. Cathcart and Marcia Tucker, *Alfred Jensen: Paintings and Drawings from the Years 1957–1977* (Buffalo: Albright-Knox Art Gallery, 1978), 7.

2. Ibid., 9.

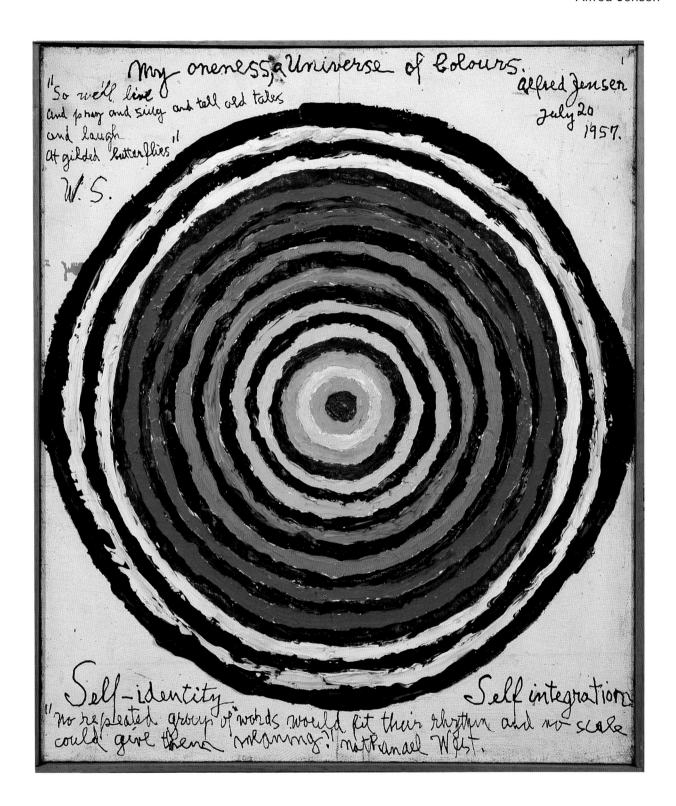

47
My Oneness, A Universe of Colours, 1957
Oil on canvas; 26 x 22 inches
Edward R. Downe, Jr., New York

Alfred Jensen

48
Entoptic Color, 1959
Oil on canvas; 50 x 75 inches
The Peter Jensen Trust, New York

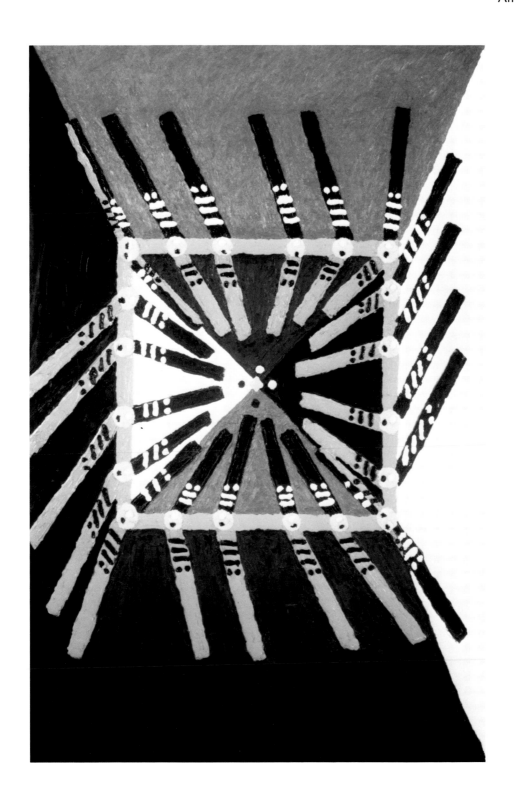

49
Mayan Temple, Per IV, Teotihuacan, 1962
Oil on canvas; 76 x 50 inches
Edward R. Downe, Jr., New York

Alfred Jensen

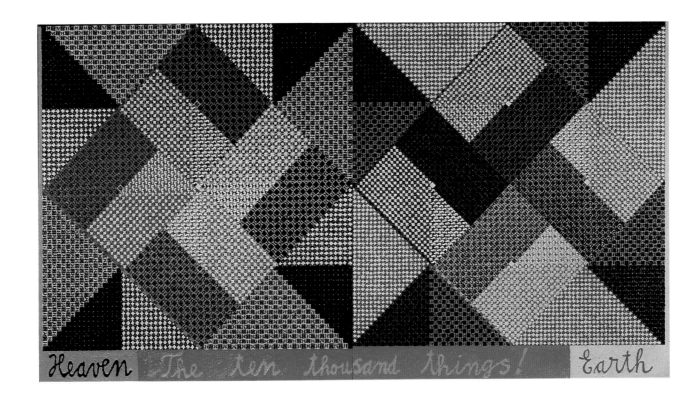

52
Heaven and Earth, The Ten Thousand Things, 1972
Oil on canvas; two panels, each 63½ x 69 inches
Elizabeth B. Blake, Dallas

Alfred Jensen, 1973

Biography

Born Alfred Julio Jensen, December 11, 1903, in Guatemala City, Guatemala. Moved to Denmark, 1910. Relocated in California, 1919. Bought farm in Guatemala, 1922. Moved back to California, 1924. Education: San Diego School of Fine Arts, Balboa Park, Calif., 1924–25; Moritz Heymann's school and Hans Hofmann's school in Munich, Germany, 1926–27; Académie Scandinave, Paris, together with Saidie A. May, 1929. Became permanent resident of United States, 1934. Instructor: Maryland Institute, Baltimore, summer 1958. Awards include: Tamarind Lithography Workshop Artist-Fellow, 1965. Died April 4, 1981, in Glen Ridge, New Jersey.

Selected Solo Exhibitions

1952
John Heller Gallery, New York, *Alfred J. Jensen: Experiments in Color,* March 17–29.

1955
Tanager Gallery, New York, *Alfred Jensen,* October 21–November 10.

1957
Bertha Schaefer Gallery, New York, *Recent Oils by Alfred Jensen,* November 11–30.

1959
Martha Jackson Gallery, New York, *Presenting Two Murals by Alfred Jensen,* April 22–May 18.
Martha Jackson Gallery, New York, *Alfred Jensen and the Image of the Prism,* November 24–December 19.

1961
Martha Jackson Gallery, New York, *Jensen: Magic Square,* January 17–February 11.
Solomon R. Guggenheim Museum, New York, *Alfred Jensen,* August 30–October 8.

1963
Graham Gallery, New York, *Alfred Jensen: Duality Triumphant,* March 5–30.
Fairleigh Dickinson University, Madison, N.J., *An Exhibition of Five Murals by Alfred Jensen,* September 25–October 10.
Kornfeld und Klipstein, Bern, *Alfred Jensen Ausstellung von Ölbildern,* October–November.

Graham Gallery, New York, *Alfred Jensen: Divine Analogy and Time Reckoning,* November 5–December 7.

1964
Kunsthalle, Basel, *Alfred Jensen,* January 31–March 1.
Rolf Nelson Gallery, Los Angeles, *Alfred Jensen,* February 10–March 7.
Stedelijk Museum, Amsterdam, *Alfred Jensen,* May 15–July 5.

1965
Graham Gallery, New York, *Alfred Jensen,* March 30–April 24.
Rolf Nelson Gallery, New York, *A Pythagorean Notebook,* October 25–November 20.

1966
Galerie Renee Ziegler, Zurich, *Alfred Jensen,* March 31–April 30.
Royal Marks Gallery, New York, *Alfred Jensen,* April 19–May 14.

1967
Cordier and Ekstrom, New York, *The Acroatic Rectangle,* February 6–March 2.

1968
Martha Jackson Gallery, New York, *Al Jensen: Paintings 1958–1960,* January 16–31.
Cordier and Ekstrom, New York, *Alfred Jensen,* February 13–March 16.
J.L. Hudson Gallery, Detroit, *Alfred Jensen,* May 14–June 8.

1970
Cordier and Ekstrom, New York, *Alfred Jensen,* March 11–April 14.
Bertha Schaefer Gallery, New York, *Al Jensen,* November 11–30.

1972
Pace Gallery, New York, *Alfred Jensen Paintings 1964–1972,* May 6–June 7.
Galerie Kornfeld, Zurich, *Alfred Jensen Ölbilder,* September 8–October 21.

1973
Kestner-Gesellschaft, Hannover, *Alfred Jensen,* January 12–February 11, and tour to Louisiana Museum, Humlebaek, Denmark, February 17–March 18; Staatliche Kunsthalle, Baden Baden, June 22–August 5; Kunsthalle Düsseldorf, August 29–September 23; Kunsthalle, Bern, October 20–December 2.
Pace Gallery, New York, *Alfred Jensen: Recent Paintings,* October 27–November 24.

1975
Kunsthalle, Basel, *Alfred Jensen,* June 19–August 10.
Kornfeld und Klipstein, Basel, *Alfred Jensen,* June 19–August 10.

1976
Pace Gallery, New York, *Alfred Jensen: Selected Works 1961–1974,* January 1–February 7.

1977
Galerie Kornfeld, Zurich, *Alfred Jensen: Ölbilder 1961–1975,* October 21–November 30.

1978
Albright-Knox Art Gallery, Buffalo, N.Y., *Alfred Jensen: Paintings and Diagrams from the Years 1957–1977,* January 15–February 26, and tour to New Museum, New York, March 18–April 21; Museum of Contemporary Art, Chicago, May 13–June 23; La Jolla (Calif.) Museum of Contemporary Art, and Mandeville Art Gallery, University of California, San Diego, and Department of Fine Arts Gallery, University of Colorado, Boulder, July 3–August 6 (shared); San Francisco Museum of Modern Art, August 18–October 1.

1981
Anderson Gallery, Virginia Commonwealth University, Richmond, *Alfred Jensen: "The Great Pyramid" and Other Paintings of 1979 and 1980,* March 14–April 26.

1983
Pace Gallery, New York, *Alfred Jensen: The Late Works,* December 2–January 7, 1984.

1985
Solomon R. Guggenheim Museum, New York, *Alfred Jensen: Paintings and Works on Paper,* September 10–November 3.

1986
Daniel Weinberg Gallery, Los Angeles, *Alfred Jensen,* January 18–February 15.

1987
Pace Gallery, New York, *Alfred Jensen: Major Paintings,* March 20–April 18.

Selected Group Exhibitions

1954
Tanager Gallery, New York, *Becker, Jensen, Hazelet,* January 2–23.
Stable Gallery, New York, *Third Annual Exhibition of Painting and Sculpture* (also included in Fourth and Fifth Annuals).

1960
Institute of Contemporary Art, Boston, *The Image Lost and Found,* May 21–August 14.

1961
Solomon R. Guggenheim Museum, New York, *American Abstract Expressionists and Imagists,* October 13–December 31.

1962
Art Institute of Chicago, *Sixty-Fifth American Exhibition,* January 5–February 18.
Whitney Museum of American Art, New York, *Geometric Abstraction in America,* March 20–May 13.

1963
Whitney Museum of American Art, New York, *Annual Exhibition 1963: Contemporary American Painting,* January 10–March 18 (also included in 1973 and 1977 Biennials).
Corcoran Gallery of Art, Washington, D.C., *Twenty-Eighth Biennial Exhibition of American Painting,* January 18–March 3.

1964
Los Angeles County Museum of Art, *Post Painterly Abstraction,* April 23–June 7, and tour to Walker Art Center, Minneapolis, July 13–August 16; Art Gallery of Ontario, Toronto, November 20–December 20.
Museum Fridericianum, Orangerie im Auepark, Kassel, West Germany, *Documenta III,* June 27–October 10 (also included in Documenta 4 and 5).

1971
Whitney Museum of American Art, New York, *The Structure of Color,* February 25–April 19.

1977
Philadelphia College of Art, *Time,* April 24–May 21.

1980
Rose Art Museum, Brandeis University, Waltham, Mass., *Aspects of the Seventies: Mavericks,* May 22–June 29.

1984
New York Studio School, New York, *"I Knew It To Be So!": Forrest Bess, Alfred Jensen, Myron Stout: Theory and the Visionary,* March 30–May 2, and tour to Center for the Arts, Muhlenberg College, Allentown, Pa., May 18–June 29.

1986
Wellesley College Museum, Wellesley, Mass., *1976–1986: The Years of Collecting Contemporary American Art, Selections from the Edward R. Downe, Jr., Collection,* November 13–January 18, 1987.

Alfred Jensen

Selected Bibliography

Alfred Jensen. Exhibition catalog. Hannover: Kestner-Gesellschaft, 1973. Texts by Wieland Schmied and Allan Kaprow.

Alfred Jensen. Exhibition folder. Basel: Kunsthalle, 1975. Texts by Carlo Hubert and Eberhard Kornfeld.

Alfred Jensen Ölbilder. Exhibition brochure. Zurich: Galerie Kornfeld, 1972.

Alfred Jensen: Ölbilder 1961–1975. Exhibition catalog. Zurich: Galerie Kornfeld, 1977. Statement by the artist.

Alfred Jensen: Recent Paintings. Exhibition catalog. New York: Pace Gallery, 1973. Statement by the artist.

Bochner, Mel. "The Serial Attitude." *Artforum* 6 (December 1967): 28–33.

Brach, Paul. "Alfred Jensen and the Abstract Absolute." *Art in America* 66 (May 1978): 73–75.

Cathcart, Linda, and Marcia Tucker. *Alfred Jensen: Paintings and Diagrams from the Years 1957–1977*. Exhibition catalog. Buffalo, N.Y.: Albright-Knox Art Gallery, 1977. Includes statements by the artist.

Davis, Douglas. "The Painters' Painters." *Newsweek* 83 (May 13, 1974): 108–13.

Goldin, Amy. "Patterns, Grids, and Painting." *Artforum* 14 (September 1975): 50–54.

Herrera, Philip. "Alfred Jensen 1903–1981." *Art in America* 69 (Summer 1981): 19.

Jensen, Alfred. "The Reciprocal Relationship of Unity 20. 1969." *Art Now New York* 2, no. 4 (1970): n.p.

———. "Statement." *It Is* (Autumn 1959): 15.

Judd, Donald. *Arts Magazine* 37 (April 1963): 52.

Kaprow, Allan. "The World View of Alfred Jensen." *Art News* 62 (December 1963): 64–66. Reply to De Hirsch Margules's letter to the editor, *Art News* 62 (January 1964): 6.

Kuspit, Donald B. "Alfred Jensen: Systems Must Agree." *Artforum* 16 (April 1978): 38–41.

La Farge, Henry A. "Jensen." *Art News* 51 (March 1952): 54.

Loring, John. "Checkers with the Right Man." *Arts Magazine* 47 (March 1973): 60–62.

Perrin, Peter. "All the Beautiful Systems: Alfred Jensen." *Arts Canada* 36 (May–June 1979): 40–49.

Schjeldahl, Peter. "Ever Intimidated by a Painting?" *New York Times*, May 28, 1972, sec. 2, p. 17.

Jess

Ambiguity and intellectual complexity enrich Jess's art. Literary references are secreted within his paintings and collages, as are images recalling ancient cultures and periods in art history. His works and their titles can be understood on several levels, and these interrelationships extend his art in different directions.

In his art Jess has a totally different objective than he did in the logical scientific world he once inhabited. He was first educated as a scientist. After being inducted into the Army, he was eventually posted to the Manhattan Project in Oak Ridge, Tennessee, where he became involved with the production of the atomic bomb. When he left the service he returned to the California Institute of Technology in Pasadena. He completed his course work and got his degree in 1948 when he went to work on the Hanford Project, which was also producing nuclear weapons. Jess's interest in art possibly came as an antidote to this involvement with atomic energy. "The direction it was going seemed questionable, nightmarish in some ways."[1] In 1949 he enrolled in the California School of Fine Arts (now the San Francisco Art Institute) "reawakened" by a stimulating faculty that included Richard Diebenkorn, David Park, and Clyfford Still. When the director and the faculty changed in 1951, he left to paint on his own and to begin his experiments with collage.

Jess's works take three different forms. The "salvages" are older paintings by himself or others that he decides to rescue by overpainting or collaging. The "translations" are paintings, copies in color of black-and-white photographs, old engravings, and other images that once graced the pages of a newspaper, magazine, or book. He applies paint in layers to create impasto areas and writes on the back and sometimes on the front of each painting. The text is from a source unrelated to the colorful enlarged copy, but the two make sense as a whole. The images, together with the extracts, give the translations an air of mystery. The "paste-ups" are complex collages whose meanings are accessible on many levels. Jess combines and juxtaposes fragments of images on hundreds of pieces of paper from many different sources in a way that suggests intricate puzzles. The paste-ups are like visual treasure chests that yield more the deeper you dig. Although the paradoxes and ambiguities within these complex works cannot be completely resolved, an intuitive viewer can glean something of their meaning.

Jess combined symbols, figures, and abstraction in *Attention Which Is the Eye of the Heart,* 1963–72 (61), by salvaging one of his own paintings from 1963. Using associative elements, he transformed the scene to invoke hills, sand, and water. A line drawing from an ancient Greek vase appears in the upper right; wild horses cavort on the left; and a diver with face mask carries an ancient Greek vase in the lower right.

The image for *Will Wonders Never Cease,* 1969 (57), was inspired by an engraving in A.W. Gould's *Mother Nature's Children.* The engraving, in turn, was based on a painting by J. Dvorak, *The First Butterfly Net,* of two children waiting patiently while a third disengages a butterfly from a net. The text refers to a story about a boy and his butterfly collection from the last few phrases of Gertrude Stein's *The Making of the Americans.* The image in *Mort and Marge,* 1971 (58), was taken from an illustration by the cartoonist Arthur B. Frost for "The Three Voices," a poem by Lewis Carroll from *Rhyme? and Reason?,* a volume of humorous verse and narrative nonsense poems. The text appended to the back of the painting is from Carroll's *Sylvie and Bruno,* a combination fairy tale and social novel that his audience never fully appreciated. Jess "translated" these works into color with a sense of California light.

The Hang'd Man: Tarot XIII, 1960 (54), a collage of lithographic illustrations mounted on heavy wove paper with a window-shade pull behind a screen door, is one of the largest paste-ups Jess has produced. The image of a flayed man hanged upside-down fills the full length of this work. According to the tarot (the set of twenty-two pictorial cards used to tell fortunes in one of the oldest card games known to Western man), the image describes a voluntary, ritualistic act of self-purification; it is not an execution. The window-shade may refer to the tarot's function of providing insight by lifting a veil to reveal the real nature of things. Interlocking figures and forms in varying sizes surround the figure, and differences in scale effectively create spatial changes. In the lower left and right, for example, faces appear that are larger than the swarms of figures in the upper right. The image of the flayed man, who has a few figures superimposed on his body, hangs in front of this odd human landscape. For the most part these figures (Laocoon and his sons on the right knee, for example) are upside-down, like the hanged man. The background figures are rightside-up. The hanged man is the thirteenth tarot card, a symbol of the surrender of the individual ego to powers beyond its control.

Winter, A Cryogenic Consideration; or Sounding One Horn of the Dilemma, 1980 (63), is another paste-up. The latter part of the title refers to a line from Laurence Sterne's novel *Tristram Shandy.* The *Man in a Golden Helmet* (attributed to Rembrandt), which creates part of the top of a mountain, is the centerpiece of this pyramidal composition that has some art world references among the array of disparate images that create the landscape. The warrior's gaze is symbolically described by an arc of keys. A surgically gloved hand, the same scale as the warrior, holds a scalpel over a piece of rumpled paper inscribed with a question mark, which is next to a small reproduction of Matisse's painting *La Luxe* of 1907. Scenes of white snowy landscapes present the season.

Jess's salvages, translations, and paste-ups transform images and words into hermetic metaphors. His obsessive craftsmanship is unusual in the twentieth century.

1. Jess in Michael Auping, *Jess Paste-ups (and Assemblies) 1951–1983* (Sarasota, Fla.: John and Mable Ringling Museum of Art, 1983), 10.

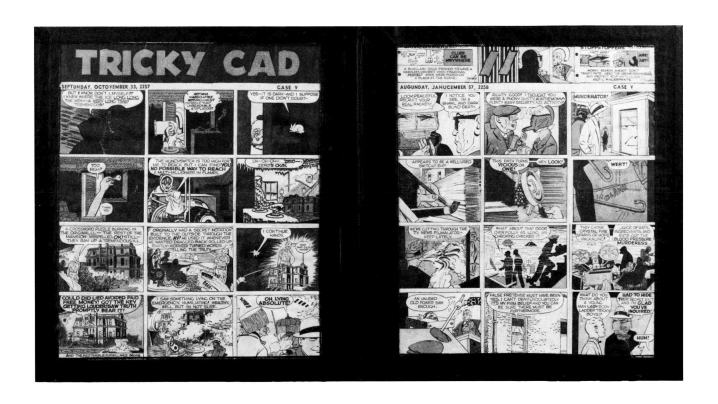

53
Tricky Cad: Case V, 1958
Collage; 13½ x 25 inches
Courtesy Odyssia Gallery, New York

54
The Hang'd Man: Tarot XIII, 1959
Collage; 80 x 30½ inches
Krannert Art Museum, University of Illinois, Champaign

55
Ex. 4, Trinity's Trine, 1964
Oil on canvas over wood; 45⅞ x 48⅛ inches
The Museum of Modern Art, New York, purchased with the aid of funds from the National
Endowment for the Arts and an anonymous donor

56
Fig. 2, A Field of Pumpkins Grown for Seed, 1965
Oil on canvas; 29½ x 36 inches
Elizabeth B. Blake, Dallas

57
Will Wonders Never Cease, 1969
Oil on canvas; 21 x 28 inches
Hirshhorn Museum and Sculpture Garden, Smithsonian Institution, Washington, D.C.,
Joseph H. Hirshhorn Purchase Fund

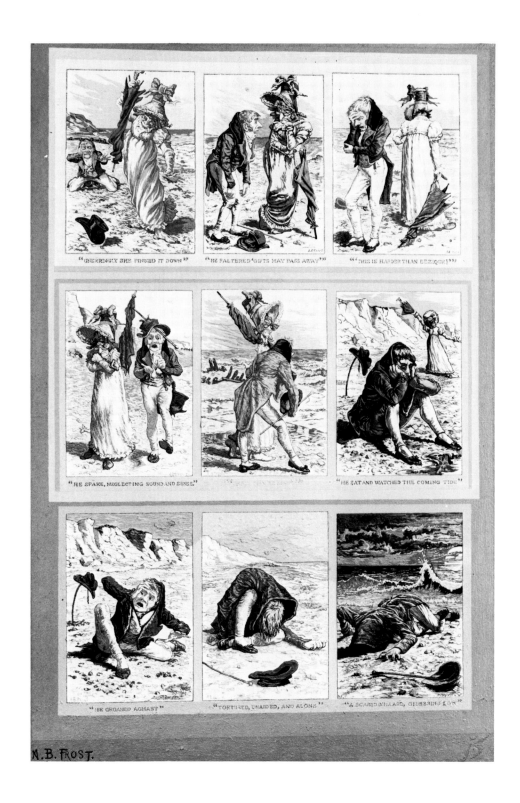

58
Mort and Marge, 1971
Oil on canvas, 30 x 20 inches
Courtesy Odyssia Gallery, New York

59
The Leavetaking, 1972
Collage; 28½ x 33½ inches
Courtesy Odyssia Gallery, New York

60
Summer, The Virtue of Incertitude Perplexing the Vice of Definition, 1972
Collage in artist-made frame; 50 x 65½ inches
Mr. and Mrs. Graham Gund, Cambridge, Massachusetts

61
Attention Which Is the Eye of the Heart, 1963–72
Oil on canvas; 24 x 30 inches
Mr. and Mrs. Alan M. May, Dallas

62
On the Way to Rose Mountain, 1974
Collage; 43 x 65 inches
Metropolitan Museum of Art, New York, purchase, and Mr. and Mrs. Alan M. May gift

63
Winter, A Cryogenic Consideration; or, Sounding One Horn of the Dilemma, 1980
Collage; 48 x 72 inches
Elizabeth B. Blake, Dallas

Jess, 1983

Biography

Born Burgess Franklin Collins, August 6, 1923, in Long Beach, California. Education: California Institute of Technology, Pasadena, B.S. in Chemistry, 1948; California School of Fine Arts, San Francisco, 1949–51. Awards include Visual Artists Fellowship, Painting, National Endowment for the Arts, 1973. Lives and works in San Francisco.

Selected Solo Exhibitions

1954
The Place, San Francisco.

1968
San Francisco Museum of Art, *Paste-ups by Jess,* May 31–June 30.

1971
Odyssia Gallery, New York, *Translations by Jess,* May 8–June 12.

1972
Museum of Contemporary Art, Chicago, *Jess: Paste-ups,* December 16–January 28, 1973.

1974
Museum of Modern Art, New York, *Translations by Jess,* October 28–December 4.

1975
Wadsworth Atheneum, Hartford, Conn., *Matrix Two: Jess,* January–February.
Galleria Odyssia, Rome, *Jess,* November 22–December 20.

1977
Dallas Museum of Fine Arts, *Translations, Salvages, Paste-ups by Jess,* April 6–May 15, and tour to University Art Museum, University of California, Berkeley, June 7–July 24; Des Moines (Iowa) Art Center, October 26–December 4.

1978
Odyssia Gallery, New York, *Salvages/Paste-ups: An Exhibition by Jess,* November 21–December 16.

1980
University Art Museum, University of California, Berkeley, *Matrix Thirty-Seven: Jess,*
    August–October.
Odyssia Gallery, New York, *Jess: The Four Seasons and Other Paste-ups,* December 2–
    January 16, 1981.

1981
Arts Club of Chicago, *Paintings by Jess,* February 25–April 4.

1982
Odyssia Gallery, New York, *Jess: The Romantic Paintings,* March 30–April 30.

1983
Gallery Paule Anglim, San Francisco, *Jess: Paste-ups 1954–1982,* May 11–June 11.
John and Mable Ringling Museum of Art, Sarasota, Fla., *Jess: Paste-ups (and Assemblies)*
    1951–1983, December 9–February 5, 1984, and tour to Newport Harbor Art
    Museum, Newport Beach, Calif., May 3–June 10.

1987
Cleveland Museum of Art, *Jess: Translations, Salvages and Paste-ups,* June 30–September 6.

Selected Group Exhibitions

1953
King Ubu Gallery, San Francisco.

1961
Museum of Modern Art, New York, *The Art of Assemblage,* October 2–November 12,
    and tour to Dallas Museum for Contemporary Art, January 9–February 11, 1962;
    San Francisco Museum of Art, March 5–April 15.

1962
Stanford University Art Gallery, Palo Alto, Calif., *Some Points of View,* October 30–
    November 20.

1963
Oakland (Calif.) Art Museum, *Pop Art USA,* September 7–29.

1965
Museum of Modern Art, New York, *American Collages,* May 11–July 25.

1966
Museum Boymans-van Beuningen, Rotterdam, *Amerikaanse Schilderijen Collages,*
    September 20–October 30.

1968
San Francisco Museum of Modern Art, *On Looking Back,* August–September.

1969
Virginia Museum of Fine Arts, Richmond, *American Painting 1970,* May 4–June 7.
Hayward Gallery, London, *Pop Art Redefined,* July 9–September 3.
Institute of Contemporary Art, University of Pennsylvania, Philadelphia, *The Spirit of the*
    Comics, October 1–November 9.

1972
Art Institute of Chicago, *Seventieth American Exhibition,* June 24–August 20 (also included
    in 1974 American Exhibition).

1973
Whitney Museum of American Art, New York, *Extraordinary Realities,* October 16–
    December 2, and tour to Everson Museum of Art, Syracuse, N.Y., January 15–
    February 18; Contemporary Arts Center, Cincinnati, Ohio, March 8–April 27.

1974
Krannert Art Museum, University of Illinois, Champaign, *Contemporary American Painting*
    and Sculpture 1974, March 10–April 21.

Dallas Museum of Fine Arts, and Pollock Gallery, Southern Methodist University, Dallas, *Poets of the Cities: New York and San Francisco 1950–1965,* November 20–December 29, and tour to San Francisco Museum of Modern Art, January 31–March 23, 1975; Wadsworth Atheneum, Hartford, Conn., April 23–June 1.

1975

Mount Holyoke College, South Hadley, Mass., *Art As a Muscular Principle/Ten Artists and San Francisco 1950–1965,* February 28–March 20.

1976

San Francisco Museum of Modern Art, *Painting and Sculpture in California: The Modern Era,* September 3–November 21, and tour to National Collection of Fine Arts, Washington, D.C., May 20–September 11, 1977.

1977

Indianapolis Museum of Art, *Perceptions of the Spirit in Twentieth Century American Art,* September 20–November 27, and tour to University Art Museum, University of California, Berkeley, December 20–February 12, 1978; Marion Koogler McNay Art Institute, San Antonio, Tex., March 5–April 16; Columbus (Ohio) Gallery of Fine Art, May–June.

1980

Rose Art Museum, Brandeis University, Waltham, Mass., *Aspects of the Seventies: Mavericks,* May 22–June 29.

Aldrich Museum of Contemporary Art, Ridgefield, Conn., *Mysterious and Magical Realism,* April 27–August 31.

1982

Contemporary Arts Museum, Houston, Tex., *The Americans: Collage,* July 11–October 3.

1987

University Art Museum, University of California, Berkeley, *Made in USA: An Americanization in Modern Art, the Fifties and Sixties,* April 4–June 21, and tour to Nelson-Atkins Museum of Art, Kansas City, Mo., July 25–September 6; Virginia Museum of Fine Arts, Richmond, October 7–December 7.

Institute of Contemporary Art, London, *Comic Iconoclasm,* June–September, and tour to Douglas Hyde Gallery, Dublin, October–November; Cornerhouse Gallery, Manchester, January–February, 1988.

Selected Bibliography

Ashbery, John. "How To Stuff a Wild Stocking." *New York* 11 (December 18, 1978): 115–16.

———. "Jess at the Museum of Modern Art." *Art in America* 63 (March 1975): 89–90.

———. "Painting Becomes Theater." *Newsweek* 99 (April 26, 1982): 63.

Auping, Michael. *Jess Paste-ups (and Assemblies) 1951–1983.* Exhibition catalog. Foreword by R.B. Kitaj. Sarasota, Fla.: John and Mabel Ringling Museum of Art, 1983.

———. "Songs of Innocence." *Art in America* 75 (January 1987): 118–27.

Bowles, Jerry G. "Jess." *Art News* 70 (June 1971): 14.

Burnside, Madeleine. "Jess." *Art News* 78 (February 1979): 173.

Butera, Virginia Fabbri. "Jess." *Arts Magazine* 57 (September 1982): 32.

Cebulski, Frank. "Lyric Art." *Artweek* 14 (May 28, 1983): 4.

Channin, Richard. "Jess." *Art News* 70 (November 1971): 26.

Duncan, Robert, introduction. *Jess.* Exhibition catalog. New York: Odyssia Gallery, 1971.

Frank, Elizabeth. "Jess at Odyssia." *Art in America* 69 (April 1981): 143.

Hale, Nike. "Jess' California Soul in Paste-up Mythology." *Art/World,* December 18, 1980–January 15, 1981, pp. 1, 9.

Jarmusch, Ann. "Philadelphia: Free-Wheeling Diversity." *Art News* 77 (September 1978): 134–44.

Jess. *The Four Seasons and Other Paste-ups.* Exhibition catalog. New York: Odyssia Gallery, 1980.

Jess. Exhibition brochure. Rome: Galleria Odyssia, 1975.

Jess: Paste-ups. Exhibition folder. Chicago: Museum of Contemporary Art, 1972. Text by Robert Duncan.

MacDonald, Robert. "Jess: Surveying the Paste-ups." *Artweek* 15 (May 12, 1984): 1.

Meier, Alix. "Jess," in *Art As a Muscular Principle/Ten Artists and San Francisco 1950–1965.* Exhibition catalog. South Hadley, Mass.: Mount Holyoke College, 1975, pp. 58–62.

Paste-ups by Jess. Exhibition brochure. San Francisco: San Francisco Museum of Modern Art, 1968. Text by Robert Duncan.

Stiles, Knute. "Jess at the University Art Museum, Berkeley." *Art in America* 65 (November–December 1977): 137–39.

Translations, Salvages, Paste-ups by Jess. Exhibition catalog. Dallas: Dallas Museum of Fine Arts, 1977. Introduction by Robert M. Murdock, essay by Robert Duncan.

Jimenez has loved animals since his childhood. They have often become metaphors for the violence ever present with civilization's encroachment on the wild. *Howl,* 1986 (70), is a strong, almost anthropomorphic, image of a coyote seemingly in anguish.

In an interview with curator Marcia Tucker, Jimenez succinctly revealed his opinion of his work's role in society. Tucker commented that his drawings show a concern and passion for ordinary people and real situations, but she noted how unfashionable such work was in the 1960s and 1970s. Jimenez responded, "Maybe I'm unfashionable in the art world, but not in the national conscience."[1]

1. Jimenez in Lynn Gumpert et al., *Early Work* (New York: New Museum, 1982), 30.

64
Man on Fire, 1969
Acrylic on fiberglass; 106 x 80¼ x 29½ inches
National Museum of American Art, Smithsonian Institution, Washington, D.C.

65
The American Dream, 1967–75
Acrylic on fiberglass; 58 x 34 x 30 inches
Courtesy Phyllis Kind Gallery, New York and Chicago

66
End of The Trail (with Electric Sunset), 1972–80
Acrylic on fiberglass, with light bulbs; 84 x 58 x 39 inches
The Candy Store Gallery, Folsom, California

67
Sodbuster, San Isidro, 1982
Acrylic on fiberglass; 70 x 62 x 257 inches
The Wichita State University, Endowment Association Art Collection, Edwin A. Ulrich
Museum of Art, Wichita, Kansas (a different cast is in the exhibition)

68
Southwest Pietà, 1983
Oil stick on paper; 120 x 136 inches
Courtesy Moody Gallery, Houston

Peter Saul

73
Typical Saigon, 1968
Acrylic, oil, and enamel on canvas; 93 x 144 inches
Krannert Art Museum, University of Illinois, Champaign

74
Young Executive, 1980
Acrylic on canvas; 77¾ x 78⅜ inches
Courtesy Frumkin/Adams Gallery, New York

75
Subway II, 1982
Alkyd on canvas; 78 x 106 inches
Courtesy Frumkin/Adams Gallery, New York

76
San Francisco, 1986
Acrylic on paper; 40 x 59½ inches
Mr. and Mrs. George Perutz, Dallas

Peter Saul

77
Self, 1987
Oil and acrylic on canvas; 72 x 108 inches
Private collection

Peter Saul, 1982

Biography

Born Peter Alfred Saul, August 16, 1934, in San Francisco, California. Education:
Stanford University, 1950–52; California School of Fine Arts, San Francisco, 1950–52;
Washington University, St. Louis, 1952–56, B.F.A., 1956. Lived in Europe 1956–64.
Senior lecturer: University of Texas at Austin, 1981–present. Awards include: William and
Noma Copley Foundation Award, 1961. Lives and works in Austin, Texas.

Selected Solo Exhibitions

1961
Allan Frumkin Gallery, Chicago, *Peter Saul: Recent Paintings,* March 15–April 15.

1962
Allan Frumkin Gallery, New York, *Peter Saul,* January 9–February 4.
Galerie Breteau, Paris, *Peter Saul,* April.

1963
Allan Frumkin Gallery, New York, *Peter Saul,* February 1–28.
Galerie Breteau, Paris, *Peter Saul,* February 15–March 15.
Rolf Nelson Gallery, Los Angeles, *Peter Saul: Recent Paintings,* November 5–30.
Galleria La Tartaruga, Rome, *Peter Saul,* December.

1964
Galleria Notizie, Turin, *Peter Saul,* April 22–May 22.
Galerie Breteau, Paris, *Peter Saul,* May 12–June 12.
Allan Frumkin Gallery, New York, *Recent Paintings by Peter Saul,* October 6–31.
Rolf Nelson Gallery, Los Angeles, *Peter Saul,* November 24–December 19.

1966
Allan Frumkin Gallery, New York, *Peter Saul: Vietnam Drawings,* March 1–26.

1968
San Francisco Art Institute and California College of Arts and Crafts Gallery, Oakland,
    Peter Saul: Recent Paintings, August 2–29.

Peter Saul

1969
Galerie Darthea Speyer, Paris, *Peter Saul*, October 15–November 21.

1971
Musée d'Art et d'Industrie, Saint-Etienne, France, *Peter Saul*, February.
Allan Frumkin Gallery, New York, *Peter Saul*, November 2–27.

1972
Galerie Darthea Speyer, Paris, *Peter Saul*, November 2–December 2.

1973
Art Gallery, California State University at Sacramento, *Peter Saul Paintings*, March 14–28.
Allan Frumkin Gallery, New York, *Peter Saul: "Custer's Last Stand" and "Little Guernica,"*
    April 10–May 3.
Galerie Klang, Cologne, *Peter Saul: Bilder und Gouachen*, August 18–September 28.

1978
Allan Frumkin Gallery, New York, *Peter Saul*, January 5–February 7.
Allan Frumkin Gallery, Chicago, *Peter Saul: Recent Drawings and Paintings*, November 10–
    December 5.

1980
Swen Parson Gallery, Northern Illinois University, DeKalb, *Peter Saul*, November 3–30,
    and tour to Madison (Wisc.) Art Center, February 1–March 29, 1981.

1981
Allan Frumkin Gallery, New York, *Peter Saul*, January 3–30.

1984
Frumkin and Struve Gallery, Chicago, *Peter Saul: New Paintings*, January 13–February 8.
Allan Frumkin Gallery, New York, *Peter Saul: New Paintings and Drawings and Ronald
    Reagan Revisited*, October 20–November 15.

1986
Rena Braunstein Gallery, San Francisco, *Peter Saul: Views of San Francisco*, June 10–July 5.

1987
Allan Frumkin Gallery, New York, *Peter Saul: New Paintings and Works on Paper*,
    September 17–October 24.
Texas Gallery, Houston, *Peter Saul*, February 3–28.

Selected Group Exhibitions

1959 Paris, *Salon de Jeune Peinture* (also included in 1960 Salon).

1961
Dayton (Ohio) Art Institute, *International Selection 1961*, September 16–October 15.

1964
Art Institute of Chicago, *Sixty-Seventh Annual American Exhibition*, February 28–April 12
    (also included in 1972 and 1976 American Exhibitions).
Haags Gemeentemuseum, The Hague, *Niewe Realisten, The New Realism*, June 24–
    August 30.
Museumn des 20. Jahrhunderts, Vienna, *Pop etc.*, September 19–October 31.

1967
University Art Museum, University of California, Berkeley, *Funk*, April 18–May 29.
Museum of Art, Carnegie Institute, *1967 Pittsburgh International Exhibition of Contemporary
    Painting and Sculpture*, October 27–January 7, 1968.

1969
Whitney Museum of American Art, New York, *Human Concern/Personal Torment*, October
    14–November 30, and tour to University Art Museum, University of California,
    Berkeley, January 20–March 1, 1970.

1971
Corcoran Gallery of Art, Washington, D.C., *Thirty-Second Biennial Exhibition of Contemporary American Painting,* February 28–April 4.

1974
Indianapolis Museum of Art, *Painting and Sculpture Today, 1974,* May 22–July 14, and tour to Contemporary Art Center, Taft Museum, Cincinnati, Ohio, September 12–October 26.

1976
San Francisco Museum of Modern Art, *Painting and Sculpture in California: The Modern Era,* September 3–November 21, and tour to National Collection of Fine Arts, Washington, D.C., May 20–September 11, 1977.

1977
Huntsville (Ala.) Museum of Art, *California Bay Area Art Update,* May–July.

1978
Whitney Museum of American Art, New York, *Art About Art,* July 19–September 24.

1980
Whitney Museum of American Art, New York, *The Figurative Tradition and the Whitney Museum of American Art,* June 25–September 28.

1983
Allan Frumkin Gallery, New York, *Peter Saul, Red Grooms: The Early Sixties,* March 1–25.

1987
University Art Museum, University of California, Berkeley, *Made in USA: An Americanization in Modern Art, the Fifties and Sixties,* April 4–June 21, and tour to Nelson-Atkins Museum of Art, Kansas City, Mo., July 25–September 6; Virginia Museum of Fine Arts, Richmond, October 7–December 7.
Institute of Contemporary Art, London, *Comic Iconoclasm,* June–September, and tour to Douglas Hyde Gallery, Dublin, October–November; Cornerhouse Gallery, Manchester, January–February, 1988.

Selected Bibliography

Abbe, Ronald. "Peter Saul." *Arts Magazine* 52 (January 1978): 15.

Applegate, Judith. "Darthea Speyer." *Art International* 14 (March 1970): 75.

Ashton, Dore. "Artist As Dissenter." *Studio International* 171 (April 1966): 164.

Catoir, Barbara. " Peter Saul: Bilder und Gouachen." *Kunstwerk* 26 (November 1973): 44.

Glueck, Grace. "Art People: Peter Saul, Wild and Funny." *New York Times,* January 2, 1981, p. C18.

———. "A 'New Realism' in Sculpture?" *Art in America* 59 (November 1971): 155.

Henry, Gerrit. "Peter Saul at Frumkin." *Art in America* 69 (Summer 1981): 135–36.

Judd, Donald. "Peter Saul." *Arts Magazine* 37 (March 1963): 66–67.

Kramer, Hilton. "Two Polemicists Respond to the Mood of the Times." *New York Times,* January 18, 1981, sec. 2, p. 23.

Masheck, Joseph. "Peter Saul." *Artforum* 10 (January 1972): 84–86.

Michelson, Annette. "Goya in Paris." *Arts Magazine* 36 (April 1962): 29–31.

Peter Saul. Exhibition catalog. Turin: Notizie, 1964. Text by Cesare Vivaldi.

Peter Saul: New Paintings and Works on Paper. Exhibition catalog. New York: Alan Frumkin Gallery, 1987. Text by J. Martin.

Raynor, Vivien. "Saul." *Arts Magazine* 39 (December 1964): 64.

Recent Paintings by Peter Saul. Exhibition catalog. New York: Allan Frumkin Gallery, 1964. Text by Ellen H. Johnson.

Saul, Peter. Statement in "New Talent U.S.A.: Painting." *Art in America* 50 (1962): 29.

————. Statement in "Painters Reply . . ." *Artforum* 14 (Summer 1975): 26–36.

————. Statements in *Peter Saul.* Exhibition catalog. DeKalb, Ill.: Northern Illinois University, 1980.

————. Statement in *Peter Saul, Red Grooms: The Early Sixties.* Exhibition catalog. New York: Allan Frumkin Gallery, 1983.

Storr, Robert. "Peter Saul: Radical Distaste." *Art in America* 73 (January 1985): 92–101.

Tillim, Sidney. "Jim Dine, Peter Saul, James Rosenquist." *Arts Magazine* 36 (March 1962): 46.

Zack, David. "That's Saul Folks." *Art News* 68 (November 1969): 56–58, 78–79.

Checklist

1
Wallace Berman
Untitled, 1956–57
Ink on parchment; 19½ x 19½ inches
Ed and Nancy Kienholz, Hope, Idaho

2
Wallace Berman
Untitled, 1964
Verifax collage; 47½ x 45⅛ inches
Dallas Museum of Art, General
Acquisitions Fund

3
Wallace Berman
Scope, 1965
Verifax collage; 38 x 22 inches
Dennis Hopper, Los Angeles

4
Wallace Berman
Untitled, 1967
Verifax collage; 46¾ x 49¼ inches
Courtesy L.A. Louver, Venice,
California

5
Wallace Berman
Untitled, 1967
Verifax collage; 46¾ x 49¼ inches
Courtesy L.A. Louver, Venice,
California

6
Wallace Berman
Untitled, 1967
Verifax collage and acrylic; 13 x 14
inches
Rodney Sheldon, Beverly Hills,
California, courtesy L.A. Louver,
Venice, California

7
Wallace Berman
Untitled, c. 1969
Verifax collage; 29⅝ x 26 inches
Dallas Museum of Art, anonymous
gift in honor of Mr. and Mrs. Robert
A. White

8
Wallace Berman
Untitled, 1969
Verifax collage and acrylic; 13 x 14
inches
Private collection, courtesy L.A.
Louver, Venice, California

9
Wallace Berman
Untitled, 1972
Box of rocks, painted, with
photographs, plexiglass, and wood;
9½ x 13½ x 6½ inches
The Jewish Museum, New York

10
Wallace Berman
Untitled (400.300.50), 1974
Acrylic on rock with chain;
5¾ x 7⅝ x 7⅝ inches
San Francisco Museum of Modern Art

11
Clyde Connell
Gate of the South Wind, 1973
Mixed media; 75 x 28 x 20 inches
James C. Bolton Library, Louisiana
State University at Alexandria

12
Clyde Connell
Habitat I, 1977
Mixed media; 86 x 17 x 15 inches
Dan and Barbara Lincove, Shreveport,
Louisiana

13
Clyde Connell
Rain Place, 1978
Mixed media; 84 x 54 x 36 inches
Laura L. Carpenter, Dallas

14
Clyde Connell
Non People Posts, 1978
Mixed media on paper; 108 x 67 inches
Dallas Museum of Art, Foundation for
the Arts Collection, anonymous gift

15
Clyde Connell
Woods Habitat, 1978
Mixed media; 71 x 22 x 24 inches
Laura L. Carpenter, Dallas

16
Clyde Connell
Pondering Place, 1981
Mixed media; 80 x 25 x 25 inches
Roger H. Ogden, New Orleans

17
Clyde Connell
Sound Post I, 1981
Mixed media; 91 x 16 x 16 inches
Randall Timmons, New Orleans

18
Clyde Connell
Swamp Ritual, 1982
Mixed media; 81 x 24 x 22 inches
Tyler Museum of Art, Tyler, Texas

19
Bruce Conner
Odem, 1959
Paper, wax, glue, wire, and fabric on
fiberboard; 20½ x 12 x 6 inches
Los Angeles County Museum of Art,
anonymous gift

20
Bruce Conner
Homage to Redon, 1959
Charcoal and pencil; 23 x 17 inches
Whitney Museum of American Art,
New York, gift of Paul Magriel

21
Bruce Conner
Child, 1959–60
Wax figure with nylon, cloth, metal,
and twine in a high chair; 34⅝ x 17 x
16½ inches
The Museum of Modern Art, New
York, gift of Philip Johnson

22
Bruce Conner
The Box, 1960
Wax figure, suitcase, tin cans, and
shredded nylon, etc., in wood box;
32¼ x 20⅜ x 35¼ inches
The Museum of Modern Art, New
York, Larry Aldrich Foundation Fund

23
Bruce Conner
Medusa, 1960
Cardboard, hair, nylon, wax, and
wood; 10¾ x 11 x 22¼ inches
Whitney Museum of American Art,
New York, gift of the Howard and
Jean Lipman Foundation, Inc.

24
Bruce Conner
Music, 1960
Film strip, wax, string, paint, Band-
Aid, postage stamp, tape, string tags,
and ink on music sheet paper on
cardboard with black velvet; 21⅝ x 11
x ½ inches
San Francisco Museum of Modern Art,
gift of Mary Heath Keesling

25
Bruce Conner
Ray Charles/Snakeskin, 1961
Plastic, nylon, metal, paper, wood, paint, and snakeskin tissue on fiberboard; 25¾ x 18¾ inches
San Francisco Museum of Modern Art, gift of the Women's Board

26
Bruce Conner
Eagles Nest, 1962
Fabric, thread, cellophane, straw, paper, photographic etching, acrylic, and ink on fiberboard; 24½ x 22¼ x 1½ inches
San Francisco Museum of Modern Art, Albert M. Bender Collection

27
Bruce Conner
Untitled, 1964
Mixed media on fiberboard; three panels (left to right): 44⅛ x 31¼, 47¾ x 49½, 44¼ x 31 inches
Hirshhorn Museum and Sculpture Garden, Smithsonian Institution, Washington, D.C., museum purchase

28
Öyvind Fahlström
Sitting . . . , 1962
Tempera on paper mounted on canvas; 62⅝ x 79⅛ inches
Moderna Museet, Stockholm

29
Öyvind Fahlström
Performing K.K. No. 2 (Sunday Edition), 1963–64
Tempera on paper mounted on canvas; 52 x 34 inches
Mr. and Mrs. S.I. Newhouse, Jr., New York

30
Öyvind Fahlström
Sitting . . . Blocks, 1965–66
Tempera on vinyl and wood; ten blocks, each 15 x 15 x 15 inches
Sharon Avery-Fahlström, courtesy Arnold Herstand and Company, New York

31
Öyvind Fahlström
Notes for Dr. Schweitzer's Last Mission A, 1966
Tempera and acrylic on paper; 29½ x 19½ inches
Courtesy Sidney Janis Gallery, New York

32
Öyvind Fahlström
Notes for Dr. Schweitzer's Last Mission B, 1966
Tempera and ink on paper; 29½ x 19½ inches
Courtesy Sidney Janis Gallery, New York

33
Öyvind Fahlström
Eddie (Sylvie's Brother) in the Desert (Collage), 1966
Fifteen movable serigraphed paper cutouts over serigraphed cutouts pasted on painted wood; 35¼ x 50½ inches
The Museum of Modern Art, New York, Sidney and Harriet Janis Collection

34
Öyvind Fahlström
Study for "Green Power," 1970
Tempera and ink on paper; 14 x 16⁹⁄₁₆ inches
Solomon R. Guggenheim Museum, New York

35
Öyvind Fahlström
Notes 5 (Wrestlers), 1971
Ink and acrylic on paper; 16⁹/₁₆ x 14
inches
Courtesy Sidney Janis Gallery, New
York

36
Robert Helm
The Race, 1968–69
Wood, leather, and rocks; two framed
pieces, each 17¼ x 17¼ x 2¾ inches
Ed and Nancy Kienholz, Hope, Idaho

37
Robert Helm
Untitled, 1975
Leather, wood, and porcupine quills;
35¼ x 35¼ x 3¼ inches
Ed and Nancy Kienholz, Hope, Idaho

38
Robert Helm
*For a Time We Were All Silent and
Moody, Even in the Security of the House,*
1966–77
Walnut, mirror, leather, and deer horn;
26 x 29⅜ x 3⅝ inches
Nicholas Wilder, New York

39
Robert Helm
*He Was Surprised That She Referred to
Her Veiled Attempt As an Accomplished
Fact,* 1979
Bark, wood, metal, and leather; 35 x
42 x 3¼ inches
Courtesy Edward Thorp Gallery, New
York

40
Robert Helm
*The Next Year, One Very Hot Sunday,
All the Details of the Memorable
Conversation Suddenly Came Back to
Him,* 1980
Wood and metal; 31⅛ x 31⅛ x
3½ inches
Mr. and Mrs. Klaus Groenke, Berlin

41
Robert Helm
*She Stared, Now at Her Gloved Hand,
Now at the Unfamiliar Room,* 1981
Wood and metal; 29½ x 35⅝ x 3
inches
Mr. and Mrs. Klaus Groenke, Berlin

42
Robert Helm
1983, 1983
Oil on board with wood inlay; 29 x
23¼ x 1¼ inches
Wendy and Alan Hart, Topanga,
California

43
Robert Helm
Coral Tree, 1983
Oil on board with wood inlay; 27½ x
20⅝ inches
Hirshhorn Museum and Sculpture
Garden, Smithsonian Institution,
Washington, D.C., gift of the Leonard
C. Yaseen Foundation

44
Robert Helm
Garden, 1983
Oil on board with wood inlay; 30 x
23¼ x 1½ inches
Stephen S. Alpert, Waltham,
Massachusetts

45
Robert Helm
Dining Car, 1984
Oil on board with wood inlay, brass,
and leather; 31¾ x 23½ x 1¼ inches
Martin Sklar, New York

46
Robert Helm
Splitting Moon, 1987
Oil on board with wood inlay, 39¼ x
60 inches
Courtesy Edward Thorp Gallery, New
York

47
Alfred Jensen
My Oneness, A Universe of Colours,
1957
Oil on canvas; 26 x 22 inches
Edward R. Downe, Jr., New York

48
Alfred Jensen
Entoptic Color, 1959
Oil on canvas; 50 x 75 inches
The Peter Jensen Trust, New York

49
Alfred Jensen
Mayan Temple, Per IV, Teotihuacan,
1962
Oil on canvas; 76 x 50 inches
Edward R. Downe, Jr., New York

50
Alfred Jensen
Hekatompedon Per 3, 1965
Gouache on board; 50 x 40 inches
The Peter Jensen Trust, New York

51
Alfred Jensen
The Hekatompedon Pattern, 1966
Oil on paper; 29¾ x 23¾ inches
Richard S. Zeisler, New York

52
Alfred Jensen
*Heaven and Earth, The Ten Thousand
Things,* 1972
Oil on canvas; two panels, each 63½ x
69 inches
Elizabeth B. Blake, Dallas

53
Jess
Tricky Cad: Case V, 1958
Collage; 13½ x 25 inches
Courtesy Odyssia Gallery, New York

54
Jess
The Hang'd Man: Tarot XIII, 1959
Collage; 79½ x 30 inches
Krannert Art Museum, University of
Illinois, Champaign

55
Jess
Ex. 4, Trinity's Trine, 1964
Oil on canvas; 45⅞ x 48⅛ inches
The Museum of Modern Art, New
York, purchased with the aid of funds
from the National Endowment for the
Arts and an anonymous donor

56
Jess
*Fig. 2, A Field of Pumpkins Grown for
Seed,* 1965
Oil on canvas; 29½ x 36 inches
Elizabeth B. Blake, Dallas

57
Jess
Will Wonders Never Cease, 1969
Oil on canvas; 21 x 28 inches
Hirshhorn Museum and Sculpture
Garden, Smithsonian Institution,
Washington, D.C., Joseph H.
Hirshhorn Purchase Fund

58
Jess
Mort and Marge, 1971
Oil on canvas, 30 x 20 inches
Courtesy Odyssia Gallery, New York

59
Jess
The Leavetaking, 1972
Collage; 28½ x 33½ inches
Courtesy Odyssia Gallery, New York

60
Jess
*Summer, The Virtue of Incertitude
Perplexing the Vice of Definition*, 1972
Collage in artist-made frame; 50 x
65½ inches
Mr. and Mrs. Graham Gund,
Cambridge, Massachusetts

61
Jess
Attention Which Is the Eye of the Heart,
1963–72
Oil on canvas; 24 x 30 inches
Mr. and Mrs. Alan M. May, Dallas

62
Jess
On the Way to Rose Mountain, 1974
Collage; 43 x 65 inches
Metropolitan Museum of Art, New
York, purchase, and Mr. and Mrs.
Alan M. May gift

63
Jess
*Winter, A Cryogenic Consideration; or,
Sounding One Horn of the Dilemma*,
1980
Collage; 48 x 72 inches
Elizabeth B. Blake, Dallas

64
Luis Jimenez
Man on Fire, 1969
Acrylic on fiberglass; 106 x 80¼ x
29½ inches
National Museum of American Art,
Smithsonian Institution, Washington,
D.C., gift of Philip Morris
Incorporated

65
Luis Jimenez
The American Dream, 1967–75
Acrylic on fiberglass; 58 x 34 x 30
inches
Courtesy Phyllis Kind Gallery, New
York and Chicago

66
Luis Jimenez
End of The Trail (with Electric Sunset),
1972–80
Acrylic on fiberglass with light bulbs;
84 x 58 x 39 inches
The Candy Store Gallery, Folsom,
California

67
Luis Jimenez
Sodbuster, San Isidro, 1982
Acrylic on fiberglass; 84 x 63 x 288
inches
Courtesy Moody Gallery, Houston

68
Luis Jimenez
Southwest Pietà, 1983
Oil stick on paper; 120 x 136 inches
Courtesy Moody Gallery, Houston

69
Luis Jimenez
Southwest Pietà, 1983
Acrylic on fiberglass; 13 x 22 x 9
inches
Private collection

70
Luis Jimenez
Howl, 1986
Acrylic on fiberglass; 60 x 30 x 30
inches
Courtesy Phyllis Kind Gallery, New
York and Chicago

71
Luis Jimenez
Border Crossing (Model), 1987
Acrylic on fiberglass; 32 x 9 x 11
inches
Frank Ribelin, Dallas

72
Peter Saul
Society, 1964
Oil on canvas; 78½ x 74¾ inches
Private collection

73
Peter Saul
Typical Saigon, 1968
Acrylic, oil, and enamel on canvas; 93
x 144 inches
Krannert Art Museum, University of
Illinois, Champaign

74
Peter Saul
Young Executive, 1980
Acrylic on canvas; 77¾ x 78⅜ inches
Courtesy Frumkin/Adams Gallery,
New York

75
Peter Saul
Subway II, 1982
Alkyd on canvas; 78 x 106 inches
Courtesy Frumkin/Adams Gallery,
New York

76
Peter Saul
San Francisco, 1986
Acrylic on paper; 40 x 59½ inches
Mr. and Mrs. George Perutz, Dallas

77
Peter Saul
Self, 1987
Oil and acrylic on canvas; 72 x 108
inches
Private collection

2/1/89 $5.39

Photography Credits

Photographs were supplied by the owners of the works of art, by the artists, or by their dealers. The following photographs are acknowledged (figures refer to catalog numbers).

Bruce Berman: 65, 68, 71; Luis Bernel: portrait of Luis Jimenez; Ben Blackwell: 10, 25, portrait of Jess; Regina Bogat: portrait of Alfred Jensen; Franco Cisterna: 55; Geoffrey Clements: 21, 30–32 (courtesy Sidney Janis Gallery), 53–54, 62; eeva-inkeri: 74–77 (courtesy Frumkin/Adams Gallery); Frumkin/Adams Gallery: portrait of Peter Saul; David Heald: 50; Greg Heins: 60; Francis Ho: portrait of Robert Helm; Dennis Hopper: portrait of Wallace Berman; Mimi Jacobs: portrait of Bruce Conner (courtesy Mimi Jacobs Papers, Archives of American Art, Smithsonian Institution); Neil Johnson: 12, portrait of Clyde Connell; Ted Kuykendall: 66; Tord Lund: 28; Otto E. Nelson: 35 (courtesy Sidney Janis Gallery); William Nettles: 3; Arthur Okazaki: 42, 44; Nathan Rabin: 58, 72; Sidney Janis Gallery: 29; Lee Stalsworth: 27, 39, 48, 51, 57, 69; Bill J. Strehorn: 3; Tom Vinetz: 4–5 (courtesy L.A. Louver); Lars Wiklund: portrait of Öyvind Fahlström (courtesy Arnold Herstand and Company); Dorothy Zeidman: 45.